Beginning Research

Researchers in education are interested in the study of learners, teachers, professional support staff, parents, and other participants in schools and other educational institutions. To be effective, research needs to be carried out in a systematic way and should contribute to what we know. If you are interested in education research, and want to learn how to become an effective researcher, then this step-by-step guide is for you. For many students the first research project is the most daunting but this book will help you ensure it is a success.

Beginning Research is a practical toolkit of resources that will enable you to plan, conduct and follow up your research effectively. It contains information on the range of methods available to researchers, and introduces some of the key concepts associated with education research and the theoretical background against which it currently takes place. This book has been designed for anyone working in an education setting. By reading through each chapter and completing the associated tasks you will be able to work through each stage of the research process.

This book is essential reading for students on all education courses who are engaging in research for the first time. It is particularly suitable for Foundation Degree students, as it acknowledges the constraints placed upon researchers who are also working, and offers practical advice for managing the demands of employment, study and carrying out research.

Michelle Lowe is Senior Lecturer at the Institute for Education Policy Research at Staffordshire University, UK.

Beginning Research

A guide for foundation degree students

Michelle Lowe

Routledge
Taylor & Francis Group

LONDON AND NEW YORK

First published 2007
by Routledge
2 Park Square, Milton Park, Abingdon, Oxon OX14 4RN

Simultaneously published in the USA and Canada
by Routledge
270 Madison Ave, New York, NY 10016

Routledge is an imprint of the Taylor & Francis Group, an informa business

© 2007 Michelle Lowe

Typeset in Times New Roman by
Florence Production Ltd, Stoodleigh, Devon

Printed and bound in Great Britain by
TJ International Ltd, Padstow, Cornwall

British Library Cataloguing in Publication Data
A catalogue record for this book is available from the
British Library.

Library of Congress Cataloging in Publication Data
A catalog record for this book has been requested.

ISBN10: 0–415–40980–2 (hbk)
ISBN10: 0–415–40981–0 (pbk)
ISBN10: 0–203–96850–6 (ebk)

ISBN13: 978–0–415–40980–3 (hbk)
ISBN13: 978–0–415–40981–0 (pbk)
ISBN13: 978–0–203–96850–5 (ebk)

I would like to dedicate this book to my family.

Without your unwavering love, help and support
it would not have been possible.

Contents

Figures

Introduction

As an undergraduate my first piece of research looked at the use of concept maps as an assessment tool in science. I simply wanted to know if we could use them in my school to support children who had special educational needs. I was convinced that using concept maps would enable us to capture the knowledge the children had about science but that they found difficult to record in conventional ways. It wasn't a grand piece of research, it never expanded beyond the school that I worked in and I know I made lots of mistakes when doing the research. Part of the problem was that there wasn't a book about research that was appropriate for me as a novice researcher. This is not to say that there weren't many excellent books about research available but I felt I needed something that would take me through the process step by step. Fortunately I had a very supportive tutor. In my role as a university award tutor for undergraduate students on foundation degrees I was aware that the need for a guide to beginning research for the novice researcher was still required. This book aims to be such a guide.

What's in the book?

By working through this book you will be taken through the process of doing research, as many of you will be required to do as part of your degree programme.

In Chapter 1, we begin with an analysis of what we mean by research and why research is a method of learning more about a subject. We will look at some key concepts that are used within research and explore how the different ways in which we view the world are linked to our approach to carrying out research. Qualitative and quantitative research methods are introduced along with some key research concepts such as validity, reliability and generalisation. In Chapter 2 the book discusses the ethical issues that need to be understood when carrying out research, particularly research with children and young people. It situates research within the legislative context and introduces you to the protocols of securing participation in research. The responsibilities of the researcher in the research process are outlined. In Chapter 3 you will be supported through reflective tasks to identify potential topics for your own research. This includes an exploration of potential sources of stimulus for research topics. You will also begin to identify the personal, historical, social and political aspects that frame research activities. Towards the end of this chapter you will have begun to develop your own research question.

Chapters 4 through to 9 are written as complementary pairs. The first chapter in each pair introduces a key element of research method and introduces you to the theoretical concepts required to make an informed decision about each method. The second chapter in each pair has a more practical focus and encourages you to begin to apply theoretical knowledge to your research question.

In Chapter 4 we explore the use of questionnaires in research. By using simulated questionnaires and analysing their effectiveness you will begin the process of understanding why we use questionnaires, the advantages and limitations of using questionnaires and the need for pilot activities. In Chapter 5 the process of creating a questionnaire is worked through systematically. The role of language in making questionnaires successful and principles of design

and layout are addressed. In Chapter 6 we turn to the use of observation techniques in research and discuss the advantages and
disadvantages. Through reflective tasks you will explore the ethical
considerations that need to be accounted for when conducting observations. Chapter 7 explores how researchers manage observations
and the techniques used for capturing data. These include observation schedules, the use of video and the use of audio recording.
Chapter 8 provides an introduction to the advantages and disadvantages of using interviews as a research tool. The different
approaches required when interviewing children and adults are
explored. Chapter 9 outlines the protocols for conducting interviews, ways of recording interviews and the design of interview
schedules.

Action research is sometimes called the 'practitioner as
researcher' model, because the practitioner and researcher is the
same person (Campbell *et al*. 2004). This would appear to be a
research method that has benefits for the researcher who also has
a professional working life, and it can be a method of combining
work with research. A full exploration of this methodology and the
methods used to gather data, and the benefits and advantages, are
discussed in Chapter 10.

An essential part of any research is analysing the data gathered. The final chapters in this book support you through the process
of analysing and presenting your findings. In Chapter 11 we explore
the tools for analysing data. Chapter 12 highlights the need to share
research and you will be introduced to ways in which research is
structured for presentation.

This book has been written to appeal to readers from a variety
of backgrounds. Consequently I have attempted to make the text
accessible to all, whilst providing stimulating challenges. My spe-
cialism is education and the professional development of teaching
assistants, and many of the examples in this book are therefore
drawn from this field. However, the key concepts and good practice recommendations are generic and applicable across a variety
of subjects. Each chapter is structured to begin with an outline of
the contents, and contains tasks that will help re-enforce the particular concepts and theories being discussed. In developing your study

skills it is often helpful to begin by reading about the issue you are interested in so that you become familiar with the ideas presented. It is then a good idea to re-read this information, making notes as you go.

In reading this book you may also want to carry out the tasks that have been included. These have been designed to help you structure your thinking in a way that relates it to your own practice. Completing the tasks will help you to think about the research you want to carry out. The tasks are varied; some require you to think about your own practice whereas others require you to produce a written response. Space has been provided for you to record your response with the task. In addition, each chapter contains subheadings that will help you find the information you need quickly. There is a reference section at the end of the book that will provide you with some useful suggestions for further reading. Don't worry if you find this a difficult area to understand at first. The best way to learn about research is to do it! Carrying out research for the first time can be daunting but it is also a fascinating voyage of discovery. Not only will you learn more about your chosen topic, you will also learn about yourself as a result of conducting research. Good luck, and enjoy your research!

Chapter 1
What is research?

Introduction

This chapter introduces you to what we mean when we say we are 'doing research' and why research is an important way of learning more about a subject. You will meet some key concepts that are used within research. This chapter also outlines how the different ways in which we view the world are linked to our approach to carrying out research.

What is research?

Howard and Sharp (1983: 6) define research as 'seeking through methodical processes to add to one's own body of knowledge and, hopefully, to that of others, by the discovery of non trivial facts and insights'. Similarly, Drew (1980: 4) sees research as 'conducted to solve problems and expand knowledge'. We can find out about the world around us in many ways. The most direct way we have is through direct experience. For example we can learn and know about physical objects through our senses. Similarly, we can experience emotions through our interactions with others. Reasoning is our second way of learning about the world. We can reason about the world by making deductions about new phenomena based upon things that we already know and or have experienced. For example:

1   We know that the planets in our solar system orbit the sun.
2   We discover a new planet in our solar system.
3   It too must orbit the sun.

The third way in which we can find out about the world is through research. Research differs from experience because it is controlled and carried out systematically. Research may be based upon our experiences and it may develop from the process of reasoning about the world. However, research has certain characteristics that make it a very useful way of learning about and understanding the world around us. It can be viewed as a tool (MacNaughton *et al*. 2001: 3). Learning how to use the tool will help you to feel confident about conducting research within education.

Why research?

The ways in which education practitioners work are subject to change in response to legislation, policy and practice. At the same time our interpretation of learning and teaching has changed to accommodate new understandings. Education does not occur within a vacuum. Education is influenced by social, political, historical, economic, technological and ecological factors. Research can help us to explore education and the education process. It can help us to begin to answer questions about learning and teaching. You will have your own personal reasons for wanting to conduct research. It may be that you have to conduct research as part of your foundation degree. You may want to conduct action research with the intention of finding out about your own workplace and improving or developing your own personal practice.

TASK 1A

What is your response to the term 'research'?

....

....

....

....

....

....

Identify any hopes and fears you have about being asked to conduct research.

- Hopes

....

....

....

....

....

- Fears

....

....

....

....

....

You may also need to respond to research directly and indirectly in your professional role. Your study of education has already involved you in the process of reading about the research other people will have carried out. Many national policies and initiatives have a research base. However, many do not! By developing your skills of what constitutes effective research you will be able to make judgements about and critically evaluate the research of others.

You may already have a clear idea about what you want to research and you may hope that your research will answer a specific question or enable you to find out about something you find exciting. You may be looking forward to the idea of working in a different way in your workplace. You may welcome the opportunity to work through your research at your own pace. However, it is also quite normal to feel anxious about conducting research. You may feel that you do not have a clear research focus and that you are not clear about *how* you are going to research. You may be concerned about managing the process and about the ethical considerations of research. You may also feel insecure about asking questions that challenge the 'status quo'.

You should remember that research is about extending or deepening what we know. If your research has been conducted appropriately it will be accepted as a contribution to understanding within your professional context. Quality research is underpinned by some key principles and values. MacNaughton *et al.* (2001: 9) identify these as research which is:

- ethical
- purposeful
- well-designed
- transparent
- critical
- political.

Researchers are honest about their assumptions and they are respectful of the other people who participate in their research. In Chapter 2 we will explore ethics in relation to research. The research approach that we adopt is usually based upon our view of the world. This is known as our *epistemology*. We can identify three broad epistemological perspectives:

- positivist
- interpretivist
- critical realist.

Positivist research

Positivists think that the world exists independently. They seek truth about the world that corresponds to the reality they observe and experience. The world can be described using measurable properties. Positivist studies attempt to test theory and try to increase the general understanding humans have of the world or a particular phenomenon. Cohen *et al.* (2000) define this as the 'traditional' scientific way of seeing the world. It implies that the world is ordered and logical, and follows scientific laws. Human interactions are part of the scientific laws of nature and therefore they can be measured. Positivists will set out a hypothesis, carry out experiments and attempt to generalise from their findings. If the results of the research are valid they can be replicated by another independent researcher. Anyone should be able to carry out the research and get the same results.

Three key concepts that underpin positivism are generalisability, validity and reliability. The principle of generalisation is very important within a positivist epistemology. Clearly this principle has more direct application in science, where if we conduct an experiment and get an outcome we can say that every time we carry out the experiment we will get the same outcome. In education research when we say something is generalisable we mean that we can use a small sample to illustrate a larger sample. For example; let us imagine that we want to find out the views teaching assistants have of the SEN Code of Practice. It would be very difficult to ask all teaching assistants for their views. So the researcher asks a smaller number what they think. The researcher can argue that the group they have chosen are representative of all teaching assistants. Indeed they may have carefully chosen a group who they think are representative of the larger group. The researcher can then argue that what they have found out, the views they have collected, can be said to be generalisable to all teaching assistants. That is, if we asked any other teaching assistant the same question about the SEN Code of Practice we would be likely to get the same answers that the researcher obtained. There are problems with generalisability. Who is to say that the teaching assistants who were interviewed were representative of all teaching assistants? Is it possible to select any small group to represent the views of a larger group? Denscombe (2003) has argued that the minimum number of people you should interview to be able to generalise is 30. It is important to remember that generalisability can be problematic but it is possible to argue that the outcomes of research can be related in a way that would enable members of a similar group to recognise problems and suggested solutions identified through the research.

Validity is another key concept. This refers to whether the research measures or describes what it says it measures or describes. There are many ways of measuring the extent of validity but it is unlikely that research for a foundation degree will require you to do this. An effective way of checking validity is to discuss your research with a colleague or tutor and to ask them if they think what you are looking at is appropriate for your research area.

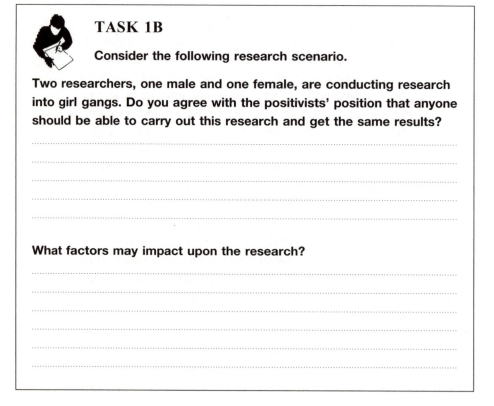

TASK 1B

Consider the following research scenario.

Two researchers, one male and one female, are conducting research into girl gangs. Do you agree with the positivists' position that anyone should be able to carry out this research and get the same results?

....
....
....
....
....

What factors may impact upon the research?

....
....
....
....
....
....

When we refer to reliability we are thinking about the extent to which the research would produce the same results if it were repeated in exactly the same way. This is important when the researcher is thinking about the method of collecting information. For example, if a questionnaire is to be used, how can you ensure that the questions would produce the same answers from the same respondent?

A great deal of work can be done to ensure that research can be replicated. However, we must acknowledge that other factors, such as gender, class, race, age, sexuality, etc. will contribute to the development of our understanding gained through research. An interpretivist approach to research considers these factors. The approach you take to reliability and validity will be dependent upon your epistemological position. If you adopt a positivist epistemology you will define validity by the extent to which your research can be copied or repeated. This is because as a positivist you will be influenced by the principles of the scientific method and you will believe that there is an objective truth that can be discovered and explained. If you adopt an interpretivist epistemology, validity will be linked to the extent to which your research is the authentic voice of the people you have researched. This is because you will believe that our knowledge of the world is shaped by shared cultural understandings of the situation (Cohen *et al*. 2000).

Interpretivist research

The interpretivist tradition views the social world as created or constructed by people with shared cultural understandings. Access to the real world comes through social constructions such as language, consciousness and shared meanings. We create and construct our world by negotiating with others the meaning of our interactions. Human interactions are complex and diverse. Interpretive research focuses on the full complexity of human sense making as the situation emerges. By exploring the complexity and diversity we can reach a fuller understanding of the real world as we construct it. The 'voice' of the participants in research becomes paramount.

However, this assumes that the 'voice' we hear is not shaped or constrained by other factors outside the immediate situation. A critical realist research stance argues that these are key to understanding the world as it is.

TASK 1C

Sally wants to carry out some research into why boys don't choose Food Technology in her workplace.

....
....
....
....
....

What issues will Sally need to consider in conducting her research?

....
....
....
....
....

Which research approach will be the most suitable for Sally to adopt and why?

....
....
....
....
....

Critical realist research

Critical realist researchers assume that social reality is historically constituted, produced and reproduced by individuals. Although people can consciously act to change their social and economic circumstances, critical realist researchers recognize that their ability to do so is constrained by various forms of social, cultural and political domination. Critical realist research aims to transform and change people (Clough and Nutbrown 2002). The transformation may be small; indeed it may only be the researcher who changes what they understand as a result of the experience of conducting their research. However, research may also change institutions and society. There are several principles that underpin critical realist research which are based upon social justice. These include equity, equality and justice. Critical realist research means that the researcher should be aware of and open to alternative views and perspectives. The researcher should ask questions about assumptions and underlying beliefs during the research process, including their own. For example, research into pupil achievement should also take account of factors such as race, class and gender.

Research methods

Our epistemology will also determine our choice of research method. This refers to the range of approaches we use during research to gather data and information. We can group the variety of methods available to the researcher under two broad headings: quantitative and qualitative methods.

Quantitative research methods

Quantitative research methods have been associated with the positivist research approach. The chosen methods of collecting data tend to produce numerical/statistical information. Some primary mechanisms for gathering data include the survey, questionnaire and coded systematic observation. Official statistics and records can be used to support the data. Further information on the use of questionnaires, observations and use of literature are covered in following chapters.

Qualitative research methods

Qualitative research methods are associated with the interpretivist and critical realist approaches. Qualitative research produces detailed field notes, transcripts of semi- or unstructured interviews and observations. Any material that can further our understanding of the social interaction being observed may be used within qualitative research. This can include novels, diaries and other forms of expression.

Much research draws upon a mixed methods approach, which advocates the use of both quantitative and qualitative methods. Effective researchers have an understanding of the link between their choice of method and epistemology and are able to select the most appropriate tool to gather the data they need to answer their research question. As we have already discovered, our epistemology is linked to the research method we choose. This is outlined in Figure 1.1.

The research process

The research you undertake will be unique to you and your professional context. However, we can identify a model of conducting research that may help you to understand the process. In the linear model, research progresses through a series of steps. Each step develops from the preceding step. You have to carry out the steps in order to complete your research.

1 Research topic identified/question formulated.
2 Research methods selected.
3 Ethics/permissions obtained.
4 Reading and literature review completed.
5 Data collection.
6 Data analysis.
7 Writing up results.

If you are carrying out research for the first time, this model is useful. However, it can also be limiting. It can be argued that

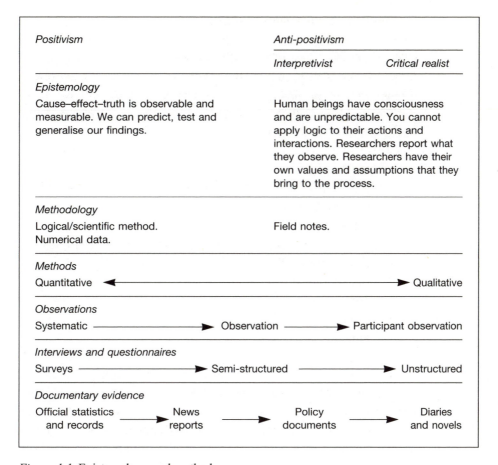

Figure 1.1 Epistemology and methods

research operates in a more fluid and dynamic way. For example, you may have already decided what your research topic is but there may be an incident in your workplace that changes your intentions. You may analyse the responses given in an interview in the light of a new policy initiative that was not in place when you started your research. It is helpful to think of the steps in research as interconnected. You may wish to revisit an earlier step or work on two steps at the same time.

Carrying out research requires organisation and you will have the support of a supervisor or tutor if you are carrying out research in a college. Your supervisor will give you advice and guidance about conducting research and help you to select the most appropriate methods. They will be able to read your work and give you feedback. Most importantly, they will listen to your concerns and discuss ethical or practical issues with you. You will be given specific guidance on the structure of your research report. Most research reports will include:

- a title page
- a contents page
- an introduction
- a literature review
- an outline of your research methods and epistemology
- presentation of your findings
- discussion of your findings
- conclusion
- bibliography
- appendices

It is very important to remember that once you have embarked upon a piece of research you need to ensure that you remain in contact with your supervisor. You must also take responsibility for ensuring that your research is conducted ethically and in accordance with the guidelines of the organisation. You are responsible for identifying your own topic, reading and methods. *These cannot be given to you*. It is helpful to create a research timetable, particularly if you have an assignment deadline. Time will go very quickly when conducting research.

Conclusion

In this chapter we have examined the principles that underpin quality research and introduced three epistemological frameworks within which you might place yourself as a researcher. It is important to remember that research is a process. There are no right or wrong answers in relation to research in education. However, there is good quality research and research that offers little in terms of developing and extending our knowledge of learning and teaching. An awareness of what constitutes good quality research will enable you to critically evaluate research that impacts upon your professional life. Knowing how to use the methods of research will enable you to make informed decisions about conducting your own research which will help to ensure that what you produce can inform our knowledge and understanding in education.

TASK 1D

You should now be able to write a paragraph that sets out your epistemology and the methods you will choose when you carry out your research.

....

....

....

....

....

....

Chapter 2
Ethical issues in research

Introduction

In this chapter you will begin to explore some of the ethical issues that need to be considered before embarking upon research involving children and young people. It will begin with an overview of the legal context in which researchers work and will explore gaining access to children and young people to conduct research, gaining informed consent and protecting the interests of children and young people in research.

The legal context

The inclusion of children and young people in research is guided by law. The Children (Northern Ireland) Order 1995 and the Children (Scotland) Act 1995 are based upon the Children Act 1989. The definition of a child in UK law is anyone below the age of 18 years. The law treats children and young people differently according to their age and stage of development and makes no distinction between the sexes. Throughout this chapter we refer to children and young people in recognition of the fact that any young person under the age of 18 may be a participant in research.

The United Nations Convention on the Rights of the Child (UNCRC) (UN 1989) was ratified by the UK Government in 1991. It aims to protect and promote children's rights through a set of principles that are enshrined in legislation. Article 12 declares that children have the right to have opinions about issues that concern them. Morrow and Richards (1996) argue that Article 12 means that 'children have the right to be consulted and taken account of, to have access to information, to freedom of speech and opinion and to challenge decisions made on their behalf' (1996: 91). The Children Act 1989 confirms that the voice of the child should be central to decisions made about the child. The Children and Young Persons Unit (Department for Education and Skills 2001) and the Children Bill (Department for Education and Skills 2004), which saw the appointment of a children's commissioner who has a duty to proactively consult children, has signalled a clear emphasis on the inclusion of children in decision making which has an impact upon any research you may want to undertake.

Ethical guidelines

When you carry out research that involves children you need to ensure that you work to ethical guidelines. Universities have their own set of ethical guidelines which you will need to be aware of before you carry out your research. You will be expected to think about the ethical issues involved in your research and act according to the given guidelines. The British Educational Research Association works to a series of ethical guidelines that set out that educational research should be conducted within an ethic of respect for persons, respect for knowledge, respect for democratic values, and respect for the quality of educational research. The guidelines set out a series of responsibilities that the researcher should adopt. These include:

- Avoiding fabrication, falsification, or misrepresentation of evidence, data, findings or conclusions. The researcher should not 'make things up'.
- Making findings of research available to the people involved.
- Reporting research ideas, procedures, results and analyses accurately and in sufficient detail to allow other people to understand and interpret them.
- Honesty and openness should characterize the relationship between researchers and their participants.

The guidelines also identify that the researcher has certain responsibilities towards the people involved in the research, which include:

- Participants have the right to be informed about the aims, purposes and likely publication of findings involved in the research.
- They should give their informed consent before participating in the research.
- They have a right to withdraw from the research at any time.
- They have a right to remain anonymous.

Adopting this set of guidelines provides us with a framework for conducting research with children and young people. If we work

TASK 2A

Obtain a copy of the university ethical guidelines that will inform your research project. What are the similarities and differences between the guidelines and those recommended by the British Educational Research Association?

....

....

....

....

....

within the spirit of the legislative framework children become powerful within educational research. Drummond (2002: 3) encapsulates this by saying that if 'adults, think of children as powerful, they act powerful. If we treat them as powerful, they rise to our expectations'.

Gaining informed consent

The National Children's Bureau identify that informed consent refers to the research participants voluntarily agreeing to take part in a project based upon complete disclosure of all relevant information to the participant by the researcher, and the participant fully understanding the information (NCB 2002). This means that we have to tell the participants what the research is about, their role and what you want to achieve by doing the research. Crucially, your participants should know that they don't have to take part in the research if they choose not to. It also means that they should know what will happen to any information you obtain while doing the research and the benefits and any potential consequences your research project may have for them. You need to ensure that your participants know what you will do about confidentiality and know that they have the right to withdraw from the research at any point.

TASK 2B

How would you ensure that children and young people taking part in your research are giving informed consent?

....

....

....

....

....

Protecting the interests of the participant

In general, the principle of informed consent should be extended to children and young people. However, there are a number of issues that the researcher will need to consider. Children cannot give informed consent as they are legally considered to be too immature to do so. A child's agreement to take part in research is known as *informed assent*. This means that at all times the researcher has responsibility for the welfare of the child throughout the research project. For example, even if a child has given informed assent to take part, if at any time you feel he or she is being harmed by the process you must end their involvement. The researcher should also be aware that the Child Protection Act 1999 means that they can never guarantee confidentiality or anonymity to a child participant where a child participant discloses abuse or where the researcher suspects abuse. Research with children and young people has the potential to cause inadvertent harm (Roberts-Holmes 2005). The researcher may not wish to upset the participant but occasionally the questions may be of a sensitive nature and make the young person feel uncomfortable. Lancaster and Broadbent (2003) have noted that vulnerability increases when the researcher is unknown to the young person. Children and young people participating in research should be told at the start of the process that confidentiality and anonymity cannot be guaranteed if the researcher feels that they need help. The choice of research method can enhance a child's vulnerability. One-to-one interviews and lengthy questionnaires may silence the very voices that the researcher wants to hear. Conversely, any research that appears patronising to the participants will not yield the appropriate results. Children and young people need to know that there is an outcome, an action or a response to any research they are involved in (Kirby *et al.* 2003).

Gaining access to children and young people for research

Access to children and young people as participants in research may be controlled by other adults, particularly when the research is being carried out in schools. It is important that the researcher has gained consent from the relevant person or authority and fully explained the purpose of the research. The organisation may wish to seek consent from the parents or legal guardians of the child or may require you to obtain that consent. Usually schools act in 'loco parentis' and grant permission to researchers on behalf of the parents and guardians.

TASK 2C

Think about the research you wish to carry out. What *risks* do you need to minimise?

....
....
....
....
....
....

You need to remember that you do not have a right to carry out research. You may find you are refused access to children and young people and therefore need to negotiate with another organisation. This can be a lengthy process and you need to gain permission to carry out research at an early stage. This may even be before you have thought about the questions you want to ask! Where you wish to carry out research in the organisation that you also work in you need to retain a professional approach to the research. You need to gain formal permission to conduct the research, explain the purpose of the research and conduct the research in the way you have said that you would.

As a researcher you are not immune to vulnerability. You will have chosen a topic of personal significance and will invest your time, physical energy and emotional self in the project. There may be occasions when you hear something that upsets you or alters the way that you think about your colleagues or the young people

TASK 2D

Consider how you would feel if you were not allowed to conduct research in your workplace. How might you resolve this problem?

....
....
....
....
....

involved in your research. It is helpful if your research has a fixed finish point as this enables the researcher to achieve closure (Roberts-Holmes 2005). You should also ensure that you provide feedback to your participants and thank them for the time they have given you during the research.

Relationships within your workplace and the relationships you have with your colleagues, parents and young people will affect the research you carry out. If you are conducting research in your own workplace you will need to show that you fully understand the particular ethical dilemmas you may face.

TASK 2E

You have decided to conduct research into the way that your school manages behaviour. Your child also attends the school. What ethical issues does this raise that you need to consider?

....
....
....
....
....

Conclusion

In this chapter you have begun to explore some of the ethical issues that need to be considered before embarking upon research involving children and young people. It is crucial to remember that you will conduct your research within a profession that is governed by legislation, which you should be aware of and which should inform your research practice.

Chapter 3

Your personal research

Framing your research question

Introduction

In this chapter you will be asked to consider your research question. You will be guided towards the identification of a research area and the formulation of related questions. You will begin to explore how the elements of a research project link to each other, and will develop an awareness of the importance of the initial planning stage. We also discuss the purpose of existing literature within research and the specific function of your literature review. Practical guidance is given on maintaining detailed records, which will be helpful when you write your report.

The role of personal experience

The focus for your research project will begin at a personal level. It is important that you choose a topic that stimulates and motivates you. Your research should also make a contribution to your

---

TASK 3A

Think about a critical incident in your personal or professional life that may act as a catalyst for your research. Make brief notes about the incident.

....

....

....

....

---

own personal professional development or contribute to the development of professional practice within your organisation. It is important to spend time at this early stage of the research process as it can be hard to change a topic within the timescale you have been given.

Very often the focus for the research comes from an experience you have had in your personal or professional life. These are referred to as critical incidents and they act as a catalyst for further action.

By identifying a critical incident and reflecting upon it you have begun to make explicit your own motivations and interests. This may be the beginning of the formulation of your research topic. However, you may have decided that this area does not interest you sufficiently to pursue it. If this is the case it may be helpful to repeat this process over a period of time. This reflective activity can be used to begin your research journal or diary. A research diary enables you to capture your thoughts, emotions and ideas about your research as it happens.

A research journal

Carrying out research will be a very personal journey. As we have seen, your research topic will be linked to your own experiences. It will also inform the way that you carry out your research. It is

TASK 3B

What is my chosen area/possible area of research?

....
....
....

How does it link to my work context?

....
....
....

How does my research link to my previous studies?

....
....
....

How does my research link to the current political, social or economic climate?

....
....
....

What could I change as a result of my research?

....
....
....

Is my research sensitive?

....
....
....

a good idea to keep a reflective journal or research diary. You can keep your diary in any way you choose, as it is not part of the final project that you will hand in. If you have never kept a diary before it can be difficult to get started. Begin by writing about yourself.

As you carry out your research use your diary to record your observations and feelings. It can be a useful place to write down what people have said to you, or to keep notes about material that may be useful.

There are other sources of ideas for research. You may identify a current educational issue in the media that interests you. You may find inspiration from a conversation or from an observation you make in the workplace. At this stage you do not have a research question but you are beginning to identify broad areas to pursue.

Methodology

The beliefs, values, principles, philosophies and ideologies you hold will underpin the research that you carry out. In chapter 1 you explored your epistemological position and explored how this was interrelated to the research methods you might choose. When you have identified your choice of topic you need to understand how it relates to your epistemology.

The researcher in Task 3C is clearly interested in whether he is treated differently to his female colleagues in the school. His professional work history has been influenced by society's perceptions of the role of men. This has had an impact personally and affected his early choice of career. His methodology will be informed by the literature on gender and identity.

Developing your focus

By now you should have identified the area you wish to study and why. An important aspect of research is developing your research focus until it is very clear. This can be a difficult process as there

TASK 3C

Read the following personal research account and answer the questions.

I work in a primary school as a teaching assistant. I'm the only male TA in the school. I've always wanted to work with children but initially began work in an office environment as my careers advisor told me people would think I was a bit odd if I said I wanted to work with little kids. In my research I want to find out if people see me as different to the female TAs who work in my school.

What interests this researcher?

....
....
....
....

How are the researcher's personal and professional life interrelated?

....
....
....
....

What is the researcher's methodology?

....
....
....
....

are many interrelated areas and exploration in one area may lead you to want to follow up other aspects you hadn't previously considered.

Task 3D outlines how Debbie, a teaching assistant, decided on her research topic. Read through the task and have a go at the questions at the end before reading on.

TASK 3D

Debbie has been working as a teaching assistant in a primary
school for eight years. She recently gained Higher Learning
Teaching Assistant (HLTA) status and is currently completing a foundation
degree. Debbie has an interest in literacy. She enjoys reading herself and
takes part in amateur dramatic activities in her own time.

At work she has observed that boys don't enjoy reading fiction.
Debbie's interest was further developed by a lecture on gender inequality
which addressed boys' underachievement in literacy. Debbie began to
read material on boys' underachievement. Some of this was in the form of
newspaper reports, some was from the internet and some material came
from texts recommended by her lecturer.

In her work context Debbie noticed that the fiction resources in her
school appeared to be more appropriate for girls. She also noticed that
the boys were reading non-fiction and really enjoyed action comics.
Debbie wondered if there was a link between the books available and the
reading habits of boys. She knew that pupils who read widely often
performed better in Standard Attainment Tests (SATs).

For her research project Debbie decided to investigate what would
happen to the reading habits of a group of Year 5 boys if they had a
better range of materials available and whether this would impact upon
their reading development. The subject of Debbie's research project was
sparked by her own observations, her personal love of reading and
performance and her college course.

**Imagine that you are Debbie. Try to write down the exact questions
that Debbie is asking.**

....

....

**How should Debbie begin to make progress with her research
project?**

....

....

Debbie has several questions she wants to ask:

- How is literacy (particularly reading) taught in the school?
- How does this link to policy, curriculum and legislation?
- What would be the effect on boys' reading if the range of books available was changed?

Debbie needs to begin by reading literature about reading development, national curriculum, the national literacy strategy and boys and reading. She will also need to explore the policy and practice in her own school in relation to developing literacy. This will give her a thorough understanding of the current viewpoints on literacy and the reading development of boys.

Of course, if we simply ask questions in an unconnected way there is a danger that our research will lack a coherent structure. Our research question should clarify the purpose of the study and in doing so should clearly limit and define the context of the study. This will help to determine the methods that will be used to answer the question. A good research question enables the researcher to maintain a clear focus. Our research question should also be broad, that is, it should link to wider political and social contexts. Where

---

TASK 3E

What is your general area of study (use topic headings)?

....

....

....

....

What questions do you want to ask?

....

....

....

....

you have more than one question they should be clearly linked and relevant to the study. At this point you may want to revisit your own questions to evaluate them. Not all research needs to have a definitive outcome, but a research project with a practical outcome is desirable. 'Educational studies . . . are a "practical science" in the sense that we do not only want to know facts and to understand relations for the sake of knowledge, we want to know and understand in order to be able to act and act "better" than we did before' (Langeveld 1965: 4).

Planning the research

You are already well on the way to carrying out the practical elements of your research. Figure 3.1 outlines the initial stages in planning a research project.

As you can see, you have already completed stages 1–4 and begun to think about the way your epistemology will influence your choice of methods. Your research outline is your proposed plan for doing the research. This is important, as it will help you to begin to organise your own thoughts. A research outline should include the following headings:

1 Aim of the research.
2 Research questions.
3 Context of the research.
4 Ethical considerations and consents.
5 Theoretical basis.
6 Methods to be used.
7 Facilities/equipment required.
8 Timescale–general.
9 Expected outcome.
10 Bibliography.

It is a good idea to consider at an early stage whether you will need any specific facilities or equipment to carry out your research. If you are going to conduct interviews you will need a tape recorder. You will also require tapes and batteries. Similarly, if you intend

Stage/Characteristics	Activities to complete (using this book to help you work through each stage)
1 Identify a general area of interest.	• Read lecture notes. • Talk to colleagues. • Read chapter 3 (Tasks 3B and 3C)
2 Begin a research journal/diary.	• Read chapter 3 (Task 3A).
3 Select a specific topic.	• Talk to colleagues. • Read chapter 3 (Task 3D).
4 Identify the questions you want to ask.	• Talk to colleagues. • Discuss with your tutor/supervisor. • Read chapter 3 (Task 3E).
5 Identify the methods you will use to collect your data.	• Read chapters 1, 2, 4, 5.
6 Draw up a research outline.	• Consult the guidelines provided by your tutor.
7 Carry out your initial reading.	• Read chapter 3 (Task 3F). Read chapter 12.

Figure 3.1 Initial stages in planning a research project

to video or photograph materials you will need specific equipment. If you are conducting a small-scale research project, typical of those undertaking research in relation to foundation degrees, you will need to consider what you can reasonably achieve in a short space of time. If you only have two weeks to collect data you will be limited to the number of interviews or observations you can carry out. When you begin to draw up your timetable you will need to think realistically about the time you have available and the competing demands upon your time that might affect your research. You may need to revise your research questions and narrow the focus.

Linking to literature

Your research project will be underpinned by reading and will contain a literature review. This is an overall review of the key literature that relates to your chosen topic. You are not asked to write a literature review on research methods but you will be asked to write about the methods you have chosen and why in a separate section of your report. You have already used literature as part of your studies and it may have informed the research questions. We need to know what the literature already says in our chosen topic area to avoid repetition. Reading the literature will allow you to clearly identify how your research links to what has already been 'discovered' in relation to the topic. A good literature review makes it easy for the reader to understand the background to your research. It should clearly define the key terms you refer to in your research. For example, if you were researching the impact of remodelling on the working conditions of teaching assistants (TAs) in your school you would need to define the terms very clearly. Legislation and government literature draw clear distinctions between TAs and HLTAs. If this were your area of research you would need to use the terms correctly.

As you read you need to keep a careful record. Your reflective journal can be an invaluable tool for recording articles and websites you discover. It is important to record the following information:

- author's surname and initial
- date of publication
- title
- place of publication
- name of publisher.

It is also helpful to make brief notes about the contents. If you wish you can identify quotations that you may want to incorporate into your literature review. You need to record the quotation exactly and record the page number. Keeping detailed notes will help you when you assemble the references and bibliography section of your report. It is sensible to have a dual system for capturing information. Bell (1999), advocates the use of a card index system, on the grounds that it is easy to carry a few cards around to capture material. These can then be transferred to the computer, which will enable you to copy and paste the information directly into other documents. This system may save you time later, as you should not need to search for missing references.

Just as you will want to record information from literature, you will also want and need to make notes related to your research. Again, your reflective journal can be a useful tool for this, as can index cards or your own system. If you are recording a field note (that is, a note made about an event happening in the specific context you are researching), you will need to remember to make a record of the date and all relevant factors. For example, earlier in the chapter we looked at Debbie's research. Part of her chosen research method was to observe the Year 5 boys reading during ERIC (everyone reading in class) time. On one occasion she observes that the boys have developed an interest in a copy of *Harry Potter* by J.K. Rowling. At playtime, Debbie discovers that the boys have been invited to a birthday party which is to take place at a cinema where they will be seeing a *Harry Potter* film. Debbie needs to record this information clearly as it indicates that the reading choices of the boys may be influenced by factors external to the school. Because her research is looking at reading choices and reading development over a period of time, it would be helpful to record the date. If the event happens at the end of the research phase it may indicate that the intervention Debbie has made has indeed begun to change the ways the boys engage with books. Where possible you should begin to categorise the notes you make. This will enable you to draw upon the correct material when you write each section of your report.

TASK 3F

Record your initial thoughts about the literature which you
will use in relation to your research project.

....

....

....

....

Are there any gaps in your knowledge of the literature? If so, record
what they are.

....

....

....

....

....

Conclusion

In this chapter you have begun to consider your own research question. You will have identified a research area and begun to think
about related questions. You have begun to explore how the
elements of a research project link to each other and develop an
awareness of the importance of the initial planning stage. We have
also discussed the purpose of existing literature within research and
the specific function of your literature review. In Chapter 12 you
will find additional information about the correct method of refer-
encing your literature and other source material in your written
report (see page 140).

Chapter 4
Looking at research – questionnaires

Introduction

This chapter looks at the use of questionnaires in research. By exploring simulated questionnaires and analysing their effectiveness you will understand why we use questionnaires, the advantages and limitations of using questionnaires and the need for pilot activities. Throughout this chapter you will be encouraged to identify research methods applicable to research in education and to your research project.

What is a questionnaire?

A questionnaire is a way of asking questions without personal interaction. Questionnaires can be used for a variety of reasons in a research project. They allow the researcher to collect information from often large groups of people and are useful for generating numerical data (Wilson and MacLean 1994). Questionnaires can provide a broad picture, and because the questions used are the same it is easy to make comparisons. A questionnaire, because it lacks personal interaction, can provoke more honest responses. However, they also have their drawbacks. They can take a considerable amount of time to develop, they need to be piloted, may need refining before use and may provide information that fails to capture an accurate picture of a situation because of the limited flexibility of response (Cohen *et al*. 2000).

Consider the case study in Task 4A.

TASK 4A

Tom is a TA in a large secondary school. He is completing research on teachers' views about TAs providing cover for lessons as part of workforce remodelling, and he has had lots of informal discussions with staff in his school. Tom has decided to use a questionnaire to gather information. He posts his questionnaire in each teacher's post box in the staff room. Several of Tom's colleagues are angry about this, and confront Tom about it at break time.

Has Tom used a good method for gathering views about the question?

....

....

....

Why have Tom's actions caused a problem?

....

....

....

How can Tom resolve this situation?

....

....

....

Tom's use of a questionnaire is appropriate. It will allow him to gain some frank views from the teachers. However, it is important to consider ethical issues in relation to the use of questionnaires. Anyone who is asked to complete a questionnaire should be involved as a result of the process of informed consent, and has the right to withdraw at any stage of the process. This means that it is not appropriate simply to hand out questionnaires and assume that people will complete them. If you intend to use a questionnaire you should clearly explain the purpose of the research and provide guarantees of confidentiality and anonymity. Tom had clearly omitted this in his research. Tom's research was perceived as threatening by his colleagues, which may be due to the sensitivity of the subject matter. His colleagues may have felt uncomfortable about expressing negative opinions about TAs providing cover. Tom should also have gained permission from his managers to use the school post system to distribute his questionnaire.

Ethical issues must also be considered if you are using a questionnaire with children to gain their views. Permission should be sought from the participants and the people who have responsibility for the care of the young person. This may not necessarily be the parents. In an education setting you may need to obtain permission from the headteacher or governors of the school. Booth and Ainscow (2004) argue that questionnaires are inappropriate for young children and should be used as prompts for conversation. Sentences should be clear and simple. Care should be exercised in the choice of words used. Remember that simple phrases of ten work best. You should try to avoid complex questions with multiple ideas. Try to use one question for each idea. If you want to explore an idea in greater depth add another question. You should avoid the use of jargon and difficult words. Remember that the people answering your questionnaire should not need a dictionary!

Respondents cannot be forced into completing a questionnaire. They may be strongly encouraged but the decision whether to become involved is entirely theirs, as is the decision to withdraw at any time.

Questionnaires can help us to identify issues in relation to the research. It may be appropriate to use questionnaires to identify issues that you wish to explore further through the use of interviews. Some respondents volunteer much more information or different information from that which you may have thought you may get.

Piloting a questionnaire is a very important part of the process. A pilot is a trial of your questionnaire with a smaller group of respondents. It allows you to judge whether your chosen questions are effective at collecting the information you want. A pilot can also identify any problems with your questions or with the layout of the questionnaire. Consider the above case study in which the researcher (Jim) is carrying out research to find out if there are any differences in the reading habits of 10-year-old boys and girls. Figure 4.1 is his questionnaire.

Jim didn't carry out a pilot study and gave the questionnaire to 90 Year 6 children. Sixty-eight responded. It took Jim a long time to photocopy the questionnaires, explain the research to the children in order to gain their response, negotiate access to the children for research and design the questions.

Figure 4.2 shows the data he collected for question 1. The problem with this question is that it is too limited. We know that 90 children were asked. However, there are very different return rates from the three classes. The data does not tell us why. Without gender information we cannot make any comment about the difference in boys' or girls' approaches to reading.

Figure 4.3 shows the data he collected for question 2. This question simply provides a figure for library visits. We don't know if there are differences in library visits according to gender.

Figure 4.4 shows the data he collected for question 3. Without the gender information we cannot tell if girls choose books by female authors or whether the choices are gender neutral. The fact that 15 of the responses listed different authors makes analysis of this question very difficult.

Figure 4.5 shows the data he collected for question 4. Jim received lots of information from this question and he was able to group some of the answers. This took him a long time. It may have been more appropriate to provide the children with a choice of responses.

I am interested in the reading that children in Year 6 do. Your answers will be used to help the school improve the library.

Q1 What is your class?

Please circle

Class 6N   Class 6P   or   Class 6T

Q2 Do you visit the library?

Please circle

Yes/No

Q3 Who is your favourite author?

....

Q4 What makes you choose a book from the library?

1 ....

2 ....

3 ....

Q5 How satisfied are you with the books in the library?

Please circle

Agree strongly   Agree   Disagree

Thank you for your time in completing this questionnaire.

Figure 4.1 Jim's questionnaire

TASK 4B

Do you think Jim's questions are effective and will help him to answer his research question?

....

....

....

....

....

Figure 4.6 shows the data he collected for question 5. The responses to this question do not give us any information about why the children are satisfied or not satisfied.

Q1 What is your class?

      6N – 22   6P – 28   6T – 18

Figure 4.2 Data generated by question 1

Q2   Do you visit the library

      Yes – 42 pupils   No – 26 pupils

Figure 4.3 Data generated by question 2

Q3 Who is your favourite author?

J K Rowling	12 pupils
Anthony Horowitz	5 pupils
Lucy Daniels	4 pupils
Eoin Golfer	2 pupils
Roald Dahl	8 pupils
Jacqueline Wilson	15 pupils
Garth Nix	7 pupils

The remaining 15 responses all listed another author.

Figure 4.4 Data generated by question 3

Q4 What makes you choose a book from the library?

- The cover is good.
- I have read a book by this author before.
- My friend has read the book.
- The teacher suggested I read it.
- We're reading it in class.

Figure 4.5 Data generated by question 4

Q5 How satisfied are you with the books in the library?

- 32 pupils agree strongly
- 27 pupils agree
- 9 pupils disagree

Figure 4.6 Data generated by question 5

Jim's questionnaire is very basic. His focus for the research is gendered reading habits but the questionnaire does not ask the most important question – are you a boy or a girl! Question 1 will enable Jim to make comparisons between the reading habits of the three classes in the school but this is not the focus of his research. Question 2 is a simple choice question, but we need to consider it in relation to the remaining questions. If a child answers no to this question do they need to complete the rest of the questionnaire? Questions 3, 4 and 5 assume that the child reads, can identify an author and can say why they use the library. They will not provide Jim with the answers he needs. If Jim had conducted a pilot study he would have realised that the responses did not help him with the research.

TASK 4C

Think about the area Jim is researching. Can you devise more appropriate questions that will provide data Jim can use to inform his understanding?

....

....

....

....

Different types of questions

Part of the problem Jim experienced lies in his choice of questions. Understanding the different types of questions can help when we need to create a questionnaire. We can categorise questions into two types – open and closed. A closed question can usually be answered fairly quickly, for example 'Are you a TA?' and usually generate one-word responses. An open question requires more thought and encourages various responses, for example 'Why did you become a TA?'

> We learn by asking questions. We learn better by asking better questions. We learn more by having opportunities to ask more questions.
>
> (Morgan and Saxton 1991)

When we write a questionnaire we can use open or closed questions.

Morgan and Saxton (1991) identify six different types of questions, which we might class as open questions that stimulate thinking;

- questions which draw upon knowledge (remembering)
- questions which test comprehension (understanding)
- questions which require application (solving)

- questions which encourage analysis (reasoning)
- questions which invite synthesis (creating)
- questions which promote evaluation (judging).

The questionnaire in Task 4E uses a variety of the question types we identified earlier. Questions 1 and 2 are simple choice questions. Question 3 is a closed question needing a yes or no response. Question 4 is a list-making question. Question 5 is an agree/disagree

---

TASK 4D

Match the question to the question type description.

Question	Question type
Do you like shopping?	Agree/Disagree question.
Which of these is your favourite drink: tea, coffee or chocolate?	Making a list question.
Young children should have their TV viewing limited. Do you agree or disagree with this statement?	A closed question – yes/no answer.
Give three reasons why it is colder in winter.	A choosing question.
Why would you choose a particular brand of coffee? Please place your answers in order of priority: Price Flavour Brand knowledge Friend's recommendation	Open-ended questions.
What do you see yourself doing in five years' time?	Placing reasons in rank order.

TASK 4E

Look at the following example of a questionnaire. Which types of questions has the researcher used?

Teaching Assistants (TAs) – from National Vocational Qualification (NVQ) to foundation degree (FD)

I am interested in the experiences of Teaching Assistant National Vocational Qualification students choosing to do a foundation degree for teaching assistants. Your responses will be used to inform course development. This questionnaire is anonymous.

Q1 What is your current programme of study?

    Please circle   NVQ   or   FD

Q2 Are you?

    Please circle   Male   or   Female

Q3 Have you studied for a degree level qualification before?

    Please circle   Yes / No

Q4 Please identify three reasons for choosing the foundation degree when you completed the NVQ.

    1 ....

    2 ....

    3 ....

Q5 How satisfied are you with the foundation degree? Please rate your experience on the scale.

    Please circle   Agree strongly   Agree   Disagree

Q6 Look at the following statements. Please choose the two that match your own reasons for choosing the foundation degree. Place a number one by the most important reason.

- Career enhancement.
- The cost of the degree was low.
- I could study at the same college.
- I wanted to stay with my friend.
- I wanted to study close to work.
- My employer insisted I do the course.
- My employer funded the course.

Q7 How did the NVQ prepare you for study on the foundation degree?

Thank you for your time in completing this questionnaire.

question. Placing reasons in rank order is required in question 6, and in question 7 we see the use of an evaluating open question.

If you are conducting a large study involving many respondents then a highly structured questionnaire with closed questions is preferable, as it will assist statistical analysis of the data you have gathered. It also enables you to make comparisons of the data. A structured questionnaire with closed questions will need to be piloted to ensure that the data generated is appropriate to the research question. This can be time-consuming. If your research is small-scale and involves only a small number of respondents then an open, semi-structured questionnaire is more appropriate as it can capture specific situations.

Conclusion

In this chapter we have looked at the purpose of a questionnaire, considered the elements that make questionnaires effective and explored the range of questions we can use. In Chapter 5 we will look at how you can construct effective questionnaires, and you will carry out a series of tasks that will help you with your research project.

Chapter 5

Doing research – a practical guide to questionnaire design

Introduction

In this chapter you will work through the process of creating a questionnaire. You will explore the role of language in making questionnaires successful and principles of design and layout. Practical tasks will enable you to begin the process of constructing your own research questionnaire. The chapter outlines the stages you need to go through when designing a questionnaire. These include a consideration of the following;

- ethical issues
- planning the questionnaire
- writing the questions
- ordering the questions
- the layout of a questionnaire
- covering letters/sheets and follow-up letters
- piloting a questionnaire
- practical considerations in questionnaire design
- postal questionnaires.

Ethical issues in relation to questionnaires were discussed in Chapter 4. You will already have obtained the informed consent of your intended participants or be in the process of obtaining it.

Planning a questionnaire

The most important element in planning a questionnaire is to be clear about the purpose of the questionnaire. The purpose of the questionnaire is closely linked to the focus of your research.

The primary purpose of a questionnaire might be to 'explore teaching assistants' views about the HLTA', but this is very vague. You should try to ensure that you have a specific purpose – 'to obtain a detailed description of teaching assistants' career progression after completing the HLTA' is a much clearer purpose which we can use to inform the questionnaire. Having identified the primary purpose of the questionnaire we then need to identify and itemise any subsidiary topics. Subsidiary topics in this example may be the remuneration (pay) of teaching assistants and an analysis of further study taken after the HLTA. The next stage involves formulating specific information requirements relating to each of the issues. At this stage the questions you want to ask begin to form. For example, 'Has your pay increased as a result of obtaining HLTA?'

TASK 5A

Write down the purpose of your questionnaire.

....

....

....

....

....

....

TASK 5B

Identify any subsidiary topics that your questionnaire needs to cover.

....

....

....

....

....

....

Writing questions

Writing questions can be difficult, but these guidelines will help you:

- Try to avoid questions that are worded in such a way as to suggest to respondents that there is only one answer. This is known as a leading question. For example: 'Do you want your child to attend a school with good academic standards that will help them get to university?'
- Avoid the use of conceptual terms, even when you expect your respondents to understand what you are referring to. For example, 'How does the globalisation of education impact upon your work?'
- Complex questions are usually associated with complex issues. Researchers should try to make it clear what each question is asking. If one part of the issue is dependent on another, separate questions are better. Complex questions often assume knowledge on the part of the respondent. If a respondent doesn't understand the question they may nevertheless give an answer which can affect results. To avoid the use of complex questions the researcher should try to use everyday language. Other ways in which questions can become too complex include overlong prefaces or an excessive number of response categories.

- Avoid confusing questions or instructions, as these irritate the respondent.
- Be sensitive about the way you phrase questions. You may think someone is old if they are over 40 but they certainly won't! You should use discrete categories wherever possible. For example, in age questions ensure that the respondent can only fit into one category and not two.
- Negatives and double negatives are confusing for respondents. Consider this example: 'Do you agree that no child should be allowed to attend after-school clubs who has not attended the initial meeting for the club?'
- It is a good idea to avoid open-ended questions on a self-completion questionnaire. The questionnaire cannot probe the respondent to find out their exact meaning. Open-ended questionnaires also demand considerable amounts of a respondent's time and it may be more appropriate to conduct an interview.
- You will never solve the problem of ambiguity in questions, but you should be aware of it when you design your questions. For example, 'Do you plan regularly with your TA?' might seem an innocent question, but what does 'regularly' mean?

TASK 5C

For each of your main and subsidiary topics write one or more question.

....

....

....

....

....

TASK 5D

Look at the questions you have created. What order will you put them in on your questionnaire?

....

....

Planning the order of the questions

A good questionnaire moves from objective facts to subjective attitudes and opinions and allows you to obtain justifications for answers to open questions and to sensitive, personalised data. A common sequence for a questionnaire is to start with unthreatening factual questions (that, perhaps, will give the researcher some nominal data about the sample, for example age group, sex, occupation). Then you move to closed questions about given statements or questions, which elicit responses based on opinions, attitudes, perceptions and beliefs. At the end of the questionnaire you place the more open-ended questions that seek answers which include reasons for the responses given. These responses and reasons might include sensitive or more personal data. You may need to ask sensitive questions. Sudman and Bradburn (1982: 55–6) identify several important considerations in addressing potentially threatening or sensitive issues, such as socially undesirable behaviour (for example drug abuse, sexual offences, violent behaviour, criminality), illnesses, employment and unemployment, physical features, sexual activity, behaviour and sexuality, gambling, drinking, family details, political beliefs and social taboos. They suggest using open rather than closed questions, using longer questions rather than short questions, using familiar words, and deliberately loading the questionnaire so that sensitive issues appear towards the end and are non-threatening.

What your questionnaire looks like

It is important that your questionnaire is visually appealing. You should take care to use a font and a text size that are easy to read. There may also be guidelines provided by your university in relation to the font size and spacing of your final report. There should be clear spacing between the questions and an appropriate amount of space in which the respondent can record their answers. You need to make instructions for completing the questionnaire clear, for example 'Put a tick in the correct box'. Using italics or bold font can help to draw attention to key features of the instructions. There may be different ways of completing each section of the questionnaire. If this is the case, remember to tell the respondent exactly what you want them to do at the start of the section. You may also want to consider making each section distinct – Section A, Section B, and so on. This can be helpful if you are using lots of questions, as you can then break the numbering down within each section: 'Section A, Question 1; Section B, Question 4'. This means that the respondent may not realise how many questions

---

TASK 5E

What font style and size are you considering using for your questionnaire?

....

Is it appealing?

....

Will you need to make any additional design decisions to ensure that your questionnaire is visually appealing?

....

....

....

....

there are to begin with, and they may be more likely to complete your questionnaire. If your questionnaire is to be used with children you need to think about clarity and appeal. You may want to include graphics in the questionnaire, or use coloured paper.

All questionnaires should begin with a statement about the purpose of the research and a statement about confidentiality and anonymity. Your questionnaire should close with a statement of thanks. It is also helpful to ask respondents at the end to check the questionnaire to make sure they have answered all of the questions.

The covering letter

You would never send a questionnaire without sending a covering letter that explains the purpose of the research, the importance of the research, guarantees confidentiality and anonymity and encourages responses.

Look at the example of a covering letter in Figure 5.1.

This letter demonstrates elements of good practice. The researcher has already made contact with the respondent by telephone – the questionnaire is not unsolicited. The covering letter uses the name of the respondent. Martin has also signed his letter, indicating that it has not simply been churned off a computer – there is a personal commitment to the research. The respondent is given the title of the research and an indication of why it is important. They are also told which university the researcher is attached to and have contact details if there are any difficulties. A clear date for return is provided and this has been italicised to draw the respondent's attention to it. This researcher has provided a stamped, addressed envelope (SAE) for return of the questionnaire. If you do not use an SAE you should clearly state where the questionnaire is to be returned. Confidentiality and anonymity have been assured.

If you are carrying out small-scale research it is most likely that you will personally deliver the questionnaires and collect them on the agreed date. However, if the research is large you may use a postal questionnaire. Cohen *et al.* (2000: 262) indicate the need

SomeStreet Primary School

Somewhere Rd

Somewhere

SS11 1SS

Wednesday 5 January 2006

Dear Mrs Brown,

RE: 'The impact of Brain Gym on spelling test scores for children in Year 4'
– Martin Smith – University of Somewhere – Foundation Degree for
Teaching Assistants

Thank you for agreeing to help me with my research. I have enclosed a
questionnaire for you to complete and a stamped addressed envelope.
Could you please return the completed questionnaire to me by *Friday 28
January*. If you need assistance with any of the questions I can be contacted
by phone on 115566 or by email at msmith@Yagooghoo.co.uk.

As we discussed on the telephone, your responses will be treated
confidentially. Your anonymity is guaranteed and no reference to your
name or the name of the school will be made in the final report. You will
be sent a copy of the report when it is published.

May I take this opportunity to thank you for your time in completing the
questionnaire. Brain Gym is an exciting new development in school and my
research will help to evaluate whether it can be effective in raising spelling
scores for Year 4 children.

Yours sincerely,

Martin

Martin Smith

Figure 5.1 Sample letter

TASK 5F

Draft the outline of your covering letter. Remember to follow the good practice advice provided.

....

....

....

....

....

....

....

....

---

to use an SAE, and high quality envelopes, for returning the questionnaire. They also point to research showing that December is to be avoided as a month for questionnaires and that a Monday, Tuesday or a Thursday are the preferable dates for mailing out a questionnaire! If you do not receive responses to your questionnaire you can consider sending a follow-up letter. This should contain the same information as the covering letter but should emphasise the value of the respondent's completing the questionnaire. Cohen *et al.* (2000: 263) indicate that first response to a questionnaire is typically 40 per cent. This can be improved by a further 20 per cent if a follow-up letter is sent.

Do I need a pilot?

It is a good idea to test your questionnaire before you send it to lots of people. A pilot questionnaire enables you to do this. A pilot enables you to check that your questions are worded clearly and identify misunderstandings in the questions' instructions. You can check that your questionnaire is visually appealing and appropriate to the respondents. It enables you to gain feedback on how appropriate your questions are and whether you have selected the correct question format to gain the information you need. If you have used closed questions you can get feedback about whether the categories you have chosen are appropriate or need refining. You can get information about the time it has taken your respondent to complete the questionnaire and on how easy it was to complete. Oppenheim (1992: 48) has commented that nothing should be excluded from the pilot and everything about it should be tested, including the type of paper you use. To carry out a pilot you need to select respondents who will 'trial' your questionnaire. You give them the questionnaire and covering letter as if they were completing it as part of the final research. You then analyse their responses to the questions and ask them to comment upon the questionnaire itself. This role can be carried out by a critical friend or mentor.

Conclusion

In this chapter we have explored the steps you need to follow to create a questionnaire for your research. It is important to remember that designing a questionnaire takes time and you should be prepared to pilot and refine your initial ideas.

Chapter 6

Looking at research – observations

Introduction

In this chapter we will explore the different forms of observation in research and discuss the advantages and disadvantages. Through reflective tasks you will explore the ethical considerations that need to be accounted for when conducting observations.

What is observation?

Observation has been described by Clough and Nutbrown (2002) as a way of 'seeing' familiar and routine events in a new way. This involves looking critically at the familiar and asking questions about what you see. It is not an easy skill, as Nisbet acknowledges:

> Observation . . . is a highly skilled activity for which an extensive background knowledge and understanding is required, and also a capacity for original thinking and the ability to spot significant events.
>
> (Nisbet 1977: 15)

TASK 6A

Think about an observation you have carried out as part of your studies.

....

....

What was the purpose of the observation?

....

....

How long did the observation last?

....

....

How did you record the observation?

....

....

How did the observation inform what you knew about the topic?

....

....

If you have carried out an observation as part of your studies you will understand this. You need to plan carefully for an observation, and it is a skill that you develop over time. An observation allows us to gather information that will help us to answer our research question. Throughout the research process we are making observations, many of which will be recorded in your research journal. There are two main types of observations that we may conduct as part of our research. These are *participant* and *non-participant* observation.

In non-participant observations the researcher is not actively involved in the activity or situation they are observing, whereas participant observers immerse themselves completely in the phenomena they are researching. Participant observation was popular during the 1970s as a method of researching education in schools. Researchers worked in the schools, teaching classes and mixing with the people they were observing. They observed behaviour, attitudes, events, etc. and wrote about them afterwards. Much of the research was unstructured, in that the researchers did not have any preconceived ideas about what they would find and let the pace of the research be determined by the situation.

Consider the example in Task 6B. Sam thinks that participant observation would be a good way to find out about teenage girls' experiences of drugs, but there are some difficulties with this approach. Sam may not interpret what she sees correctly. She may find it difficult to remain detached from the situation in order to be able to write an objective account. We all have preconceived ideas that are a product of our own gender, age, social class and life experiences, etc. These experiences inform what we think we are observing (Weedon 1987, Lather 1991). It may also be difficult for Sam to 'fit in' to this group. The group may modify their behaviour as a result of Sam's presence. Sam may not be able to gain informed consent from the participants and she would find it difficult to give guarantees of anonymity and confidentiality, particularly if she discovered something problematic, for example if one of the girls was taking drugs. However, it would be possible for Sam to conduct a non-participant observation.

TASK 6B

Sam, a 28-year-old student, has decided to look at what Year 11 girls think of drug education in their school. She is considering participant observation as a way of gathering data. What would you advise Sam to do?

....

....

....

....

....

Kevin works in a primary school and is observing the rewards given by the teacher to children as part of his research project on effective support strategies for pupils with special educational needs. It is the first time Kevin has observed this teacher and he is shocked by what he sees. The teacher isolates the pupils with SEN in a separate part of the classroom and gives few rewards. When he writes his report, Kevin writes about the observation. The teacher is upset when she reads Kevin's report and does not feel that his report is accurate. She dismisses his research as 'a load of rubbish'.

Figure 6.1 Case study

The quality of an observation is dependent upon the ability of the observer to be open to what they see. This means looking critically at situations but it also means much more. Consider the case study in Figure 6.1.

It would be easy to jump to conclusions and identify this teacher as a poor teacher. However, Kevin, whilst looking critically and writing about the event critically, has not sought to triangulate (or check) the observation. He has not discussed the observation with the teacher or sought to check that this is the usual practice for the class. It later transpires that the teacher is following advice from the educational psychologist who has recommended removing all distractions from the group in order to aid their concentration. The reward for this group is to sit away from the class and be trusted to complete the work on their own. The group are proud that they can be treated like the other pupils and allowed to work without constant supervision. It is important that we look for other sources of evidence before we make assertions in our research. If Kevin had been open to asking why this teacher was not behaving as he expected her to, he might not have made this mistake.

We can also refer to observations as structured or unstructured. A participant observation, as we have seen, is generally unstructured. There is no set focus for the observation, no agenda for the researcher to follow, but it is still planned. A structured observation, in contrast to an unstructured observation, is planned in advance and the researcher has a clear idea about what, when, how and why they wish to observe. The focus of the observation will be linked to the research questions. There are several tools we can use to structure an observation, which are explored in Chapter 7 (see page 67).

You will be carrying out informal observations whenever you are in the setting where you are conducting your research. This type of observation is unplanned but can be just as helpful. You will observe conversations, actions and reactions to events. It is acceptable to record all of these in your research journal as they will provide you with contextual information for your research. It is important to know the context of your research setting. You will know from your own experience that all workplaces are different and that they are shaped by their own history, economics, politics and social arrangements.

TASK 6C

Write a pen portrait of the workplace you will carry your research out in.

....

....

....

....

Task 6C suggests writing a pen portrait of the workplace where you will be carrying out your research. In your pen portrait you may have identified some of the following:

- number of employees
- gender balance
- ethnic mix
- geographical location
- economic characteristics.

All of these are important characteristics of the organisation and will inform your research. It is helpful to include a description of the setting in your final research report.

Conclusion

In this chapter you have been introduced to the difference between participant and non-participant observations, and we have discussed the advantages and disadvantages of each form. We have outlined the difference between structured and unstructured observation. In Chapter 7 we will look at the techniques for recording data through observations.

Chapter 7

Doing research –
managing observations

Introduction

In this chapter we will look at the techniques for managing observations. We will explore the need to thoroughly plan observations and consider the advantages and disadvantages of a range of recording strategies. You will work through a series of reflective tasks that will enable you to apply the techniques for observation in your own research.

Observing

Before reading on, complete Task 7A. It is unlikely that you have been able to write three fully detailed accounts about what you did. Writing about today was probably much easier than writing about last month, which may have been difficult to remember. How much detail did you include? How did you know what to include and what to leave out? Irrespective of the type of research we are

TASK 7A

Write down detailed notes about what you did between the hours of 10 a.m. and 11 a.m. today.

....
....
....
....

Write down detailed notes about what you did between 10 a.m. and 11 a.m. two weeks ago.

....
....
....
....

Write down what you did between 10 a.m. and 11 a.m. one month ago.

....
....
....
....

conducting, we need to keep detailed, accurate records about what we observe and do. Much of this will be contained in your research journal. Observations follow the same principle. If we don't have an appropriate method of recording what we observe, we are likely to forget. Look at the example in Task 7B.

The timing of an observation is important. If you are carrying out a non-participant observation you should make sure that you are free to observe. Tara was supposed to be working at the same time as observing. It is likely that she missed some very important aspects of the play scenario she was observing. Tara herself says that there was 'so much going on'. Tara has not recorded the

TASK 7B

Tara works in a busy primary school where she is also carrying out her research. She has kept a research journal. Tara decides to observe a group of reception children at play. This is the account she wrote in her journal.

What a disaster. I should really have agreed with Miss X that I wouldn't try to supervise the blue group with their painting and also observe green group playing with the construction toys. It was OK until I needed to clean up the spilt paint. Green group were interesting, though – J dominated B throughout. I wonder what would have happened if they were playing with different toys? They were so noisy – I only heard half of what they said while they played. There was so much going on! S took herself off to play with the sand pit – I wonder why she did that? I should have written down what J said – it might have helped me to work out why B doesn't fight back.

What mistakes did Tara make?

....

....

....

....

....

observation and has difficulty recalling what was said by an individual child. Her observation lacks structure. In the rest of this chapter we will look at ways in which you can carry out a structured observation successfully.

Planning and timing

The first rule of structured observations is to plan a time for them to happen. This time may need to be negotiated with people in the environment you are researching. It would be unwise to carry out an observation without doing this, particularly if you are also meant to be working. Ideally you should be free from all of your work duties when observing. This brings us to the second consideration, of frequency. In a small-scale research project it is unlikely that you will want to carry out more than three observations. If an observation prevents you from working you need to negotiate how many observations you can reasonably do. The third thing to consider is the length of each observation. The length of the observation will be linked to the focus of your observation. If you were looking at the behaviour of children following a reward it might be more appropriate to carry out several short observations throughout the day rather than one long observation. However, if you wanted to look at the range of communication strategies a child is using you may want to observe for an extended period of time.

Before you can plan the time of the observation you need to think about the focus for the observation. This involves answering two key questions: What do you need to know? and Why do you need to know it?

TASK 7C

Think about your own research. What information do you need to obtain if you carry out an observation?

....

....

....

....

How will this help you to answer your question?

....

....

....

....

TASK 7D

Outline and justify your plans for observation.

....

....

....

....

....

....

Ethical considerations

Before you conduct any observations you need to consider the ethical implications. Will any of the people you observe be harmed as a result of the observation? What safeguards will you put in place to ensure this? You must ensure that you have the necessary permissions to carry out an observation, particularly if that observation involves children and young people. As we have already

TASK 7E

What permissions do you need to obtain to carry out an observation?

....

....

....

....

....

Are there any ethical considerations that apply to the observation?

....

....

....

....

....

discussed this will involve ensuring that the participants understand the purpose of the observation, how it will be conducted, their right to confidentiality and anonymity and their right to withdraw.

Collecting information

Having decided when you will observe and what you will observe, you now need to think about how you will record the observation. There are several ways we can record an observation, but before you choose a method you need to think about what exactly you wish to record. You cannot record everything that happens. Bell (1999) refers to the following as possibilities for the observation focus:

- the content
- the process
- the interactions between individuals
- the nature of the contributions
- another specific aspect.

TASK 7F

What will your observation focus be?

....

....

....

....

....

Video recording

This is an excellent method for recording exactly what happens. It can be played back at a later date and allows the researcher to critically analyse the observation. However, video recording involves the use of expensive equipment. It can also be intrusive. The transcription of video footage can be time-consuming. The individuals you are observing may change their behaviour as a result of the video equipment. If you want to video children or young people there are particular ethical considerations. You must obtain parental permission and the permission of adult research participants.

Audio recording

Audio recording means using an audio recording device to keep a record of what is said. As with video recording, the advantage is that you have a permanent record of the observation that you can critically analyse at any point in the future. The same permission requirements apply to audio recording. The drawback with an audio recording is that it doesn't capture other important elements of an observation, such as non-verbal communication. Audio recording is a very good technique when it is combined with other ways of recording the observation, such as observation schedules, tally counting, event sampling, observational diagramming and interaction process analysis.

Interaction process analysis

Many of the systems of recording observations are based upon a technique devised by Bales (1950) known as interaction process analysis. Attempting to describe the behaviour of individuals in groups, Bales created a method of coding behaviour into twelve categories that enabled the observer to record what they saw. In 1970 Flanders devised a system of coding student teacher interactions against ten categories. The difficulty with many systems is their complexity. The Flanders system required an observation against the ten categories to be made every three seconds!

Event sampling

Event sampling refers to observations where the researcher records incidents of a specific event. This type of observation tends to be used when the focus is on behaviour exhibited by individuals. The researcher keeps long-hand notes of each time the behaviour occurs. The difficulty with this method of observation in a busy classroom lies in the fact that some behaviour may be missed. It is also time-consuming. The advantages are that it clearly focuses on the specific aspect the researcher wants to investigate.

Observation schedules

An observation schedule helps you to focus on specific aspects of a situation and record information against each item. The researcher can ignore other aspects of the observation as they are not related to the focus of the research. Figure 7.1 is an example of an observation schedule where the researcher has identified specific focus points.

It is possible to create an observation schedule that is more general, as the example in Figure 7.2 demonstrates. In this example the researcher has coded the children's names using only their initials. This saves time during the observation and can protect the identity of those being observed.

Tally counting

If your observation involves the recording of lots of instances of specific behaviours you may want to use a simple tally chart such as the one in Figure 7.3. In this example Jenny had decided to look at the behaviour exhibited by a group of pupils with SEN in Year 7. She decides a tally chart is the best way of collecting the data from the observation. The drawback of a tally chart method of recording what you observe is that it doesn't provide you with important contextual information that may help to explain the occurrence you have observed.

Foundation degree for teaching assistants – science in the curriculum research project

OBSERVATION SCHEDULE

Date of observation: _____

Title of activity: _____

Area of science/technology (related to relevant curriculum document: P.O.S, unit, etc.) _____

OVERVIEW

Year group: _____

Age of learners being observed: _____

Setting (classroom, playground, wet area, etc.): _____

_____

Previous experience of learners (no. of sessions in topic/area prior to this session, related work in other areas, etc.): _____

_____

THE LESSON

Consider:

What science/technology activity was taking place? _____

How did it relate to other areas of the curriculum? _____

The learners:

Were the learners actively engaged with the activity? Explain your answer/comments. _____

_____

How was the activity being taught? Active/didactic learning? _____

_____

What effect did this have on the learners? _____

_____

Did the learners have any misconceptions? _____

_____

How were these corrected? _____

_____

Figure 7.1 Observation schedule

Foundation degree in early years and childcare – talk in Year 1

RESEARCH OBSERVATION SCHEDULE

Date of observation:

Place of observation:

Time	Individuals present	What is happening?	What is being said?
11.00	JH , PT , RD	Children are playing with building blocks JH banging bricks together	La la la (JH) Shut up silly (PT)
11.10	ML joins group	ML begins to collect all of the yellow bricks	Lellow , lellow bricks (ML)

Figure 7.2 Observation schedule – general

Observational diagrams

It may be helpful when you observe to create a simple diagram of the situation. This is particularly helpful if your research is in schools. The diagram will serve to remind you later of the layout of the room. This is important, as the layout of the room may have impacted upon what you observed.

As with questionnaires, which we discussed in Chapters 4 and 5, you will need to pilot your chosen method of observation and recording. After you have conducted the pilot, discuss the outcomes with a critical friend and amend your plans if necessary. Remember that time invested at the planning stage will ensure that your research runs smoothly.

Whichever method of recording the observation you choose, you will generate data. This will be in document format and may also be in audio and video format. You should ensure that you keep

Behaviour	Occurrence
Calling out	ⅦⅦ ⅦⅦ
Getting out of seat	ⅦⅦ ⅦⅦ |
Messing with another child	||||
Messing with an object	ⅦⅦ

Figure 7.3 Tally count

that data safe and secure. Your university will provide you with guidelines on storing data securely. This data will need to be analysed thoroughly, and guidance on how to do this is provided in Chapter 11. You should ensure that your data is ready to be analysed. This will mean transcribing audio and video material and ensuring that you have all of your observation notes available.

Transcribing

This refers to the process of turning the audio or video recording into a written record of what happened and was said. This is a lengthy process, but it is hugely rewarding. Often your analysis of the observation will need to be carried out systematically, and a printed version can be easier to work with as you can make notes

---

TASK 7G

Which method of recording your observation is the most appropriate and why?

....
....
....
....

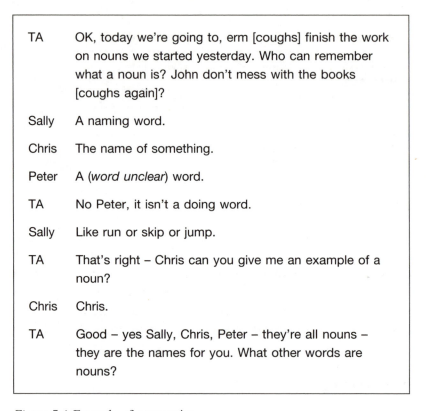

TA	OK, today we're going to, erm [coughs] finish the work on nouns we started yesterday. Who can remember what a noun is? John don't mess with the books [coughs again]?
Sally	A naming word.
Chris	The name of something.
Peter	A (*word unclear*) word.
TA	No Peter, it isn't a doing word.
Sally	Like run or skip or jump.
TA	That's right – Chris can you give me an example of a noun?
Chris	Chris.
TA	Good – yes Sally, Chris, Peter – they're all nouns – they are the names for you. What other words are nouns?

Figure 7.4 Example of a transcript

on it. Figure 7.4 provides an example of just one minute of audio tape that has been transcribed.

To transcribe audio tape, play the audio recording for a short time and then type what you have heard. It is best to only play the recording for a short time. As you can see from Figure 7.4 the transcript places each new speaker on a new line. Where the TA coughs this is indicated. You would indicate any audible noise. When a word cannot be heard clearly this is indicated. It can also be helpful to number the lines in a transcript.

TASK 7H

Record yourself having a conversation for five minutes.
Transcribe the recording. How long did it take to transcribe?

....

....

Conclusion

In this chapter we have looked at a range of methods for carrying out an observation. We have identified the need to plan for an observation carefully and to match the observation method selected to the research question. In the next chapter we will look at interviews as a method of carrying out research.

Chapter 8
Looking at research –
interviews

Introduction

This chapter introduces you to the advantages and disadvantages of using interviews as a research tool. We will identify what an interview is and how it differs from conversation. We will look at the different types of interview and ways in which the researcher can get the most productive data. The different approaches required when interviewing children and adults are explored and ethical issues are considered.

What is an interview?

Moser and Kalton (1971) describe an interview as a conversation between the researcher and the respondent with the aim of gaining certain information from the respondent. Wiseman and Aron (1972) liken it to a fishing trip. An interview is a two-way process – a conversation between the researcher and the respondent. It is not,

TASK 8A

What is the difference between an interview and a chat?

....

....

....

....

....

however, like talking to your colleagues at work or exchanging ideas in a lesson. This is because an interview has been planned in advance by the researcher.

The interview has several elements that need to be planned. First there are the questions that you want to ask, then the order that you will ask the questions. You need to select the people you want to interview and gain their informed consent. You need to arrange somewhere for the interviews to take place and decide how you will record what is said. Finally you need to transcribe and analyse the interviews in relation to your overall research question. This makes an interview very similar to a questionnaire but it has the added advantage that the researcher can interact with the respondent. You will be able to probe ideas, follow up lines of enquiry, react to the respondent's emotions and investigate aspects of a response that could be hidden in a questionnaire response.

The purpose of an interview can be to gather information related to the research question. It can be used to test a hypothesis or it can be used to follow up unexpected results or to triangulate with other methods, such as an observation. Bell (1999: 135) describes an interview as yielding 'rich material' which 'can often put the flesh on the bones of questionnaire responses'. This of course places responsibility on the researcher for ensuring that the interview is conducted ethically. The interview moves away from seeing the human subjects of research as external – the research process is done to them, towards viewing them as active participants in the process of knowledge creation (Kvale 1996: 11, cited in Cohen *et al.* 2000). Kitwood (1977, cited in Cohen *et al.* 2000) identified three conceptions we can hold of an interview. First we can see it as a means of information transfer and collection. Second we can see it as an interaction between two people, governed by theories of motivation. In both cases the respondents and interviewers have biases, emotions, overt and subconscious needs which the researcher needs to try to overcome through careful design and execution of the interview.

Kitwood's third conception of the interview sees it as having many features in common with everyday life. Woods (1986) identifies these as trust, curiosity and naturalness. There has to be trust between the researcher and the respondent that goes beyond the simple remit of the research. This is determined by factors outside of the research, such as pursuit of a common aim. The desire to know or be curious also needs to underpin the research, and the researcher needs to ensure that the respondent feels that the interview is a natural situation.

Cicourel (1964) identified five features of interview situations that caused difficulties for researchers. First, there will be variation between each interview, even when the same questions were used. Second, there are inherent power relationships in an interview which can leave respondents feeling uneasy. Third, both the researcher and the respondent will hold back some of their knowledge as part of the power relationship. Fourth, it is difficult to construct a shared framework for understanding meaning. Fifth, the researcher is unable to control all aspects of the interview encounter.

However, if we adopt Kitwood's third conception of the interview, many of the unavoidable features of an interview situation identified by Cicourel (1964) cease to be problematic. The researcher may try to be systematic and objective but should acknowledge the subjectivity of the interview as a method.

Types of interview

Grebenik and Moser (1962: 16) refer to a 'continuum of formality' to distinguish between the different types of interview, ranging from unstructured conversations shaped by the interaction between the researcher and the respondent to a formal, structured interview shaped by predetermined questions that are not deviated from.

We can identify interviews as:

- structured with a pre-designed set of questions that should be followed exactly
- semi-structured with a set of questions to guide the interview but where the researcher is free to follow up responses to the questions
- unstructured interviews, where the researcher and interviewer talk but do not follow a predetermined schedule
- focus group interviews where multiple respondents develop ideas which the researcher records
- group interviews where a group of people respond to specific questions asked by the researcher.

TASK 8B

Place the interview types described above on the 'continuum of formality'.

Formal ←—————————————————————→ **Informal**

Group interviews

The group interview has been identified as very helpful in educational research (Watts and Ebbutt 1987) where a group of people have been working on a common purpose for some time, or where it is important that views are shared. This interview type can generate a wider range of responses than individual interviews. Bogdan and Biklen (1982: 10) argue that these interviews are helpful at the beginning of research as they help to identify potential lines of enquiry. A group interview has practical advantages.

It is cost effective as it can be carried out faster than individual interviews, and it can help some respondents feel more secure and less vulnerable in an interview situation. There are disadvantages to a group interview. The size of the group is an issue – too large and there is a danger that individual voices will not be heard, too small and respondents may not readily share information. The composition of the group is also important – there should be a common feature which links the respondents together, and group dynamics need to be carefully considered.

Focus group interviews

Focus group interviews position the researcher as a facilitator of the discussion. The reliance is on the interaction between the group members rather than between the group and the researcher. The use of focus groups has grown in recent years and they are now widely used to inform commercial and political decision making. The advantages of using a focus group lie in the ability of the group to generate data that can determine a future course of action or generate a new hypothesis to test. They are also useful in gathering responses to previous initiatives. A focus group interview can be used to triangulate data from other methods, such as individual interviews of observations. If you are intending to use a focus group you need to ensure that you select the participants with care. They should all share experience of the phenomena you are researching. Chairing such a session requires some skill. The session should be carefully timed and group size must be considered. Clearly, the group interview and the focus group interviews would therefore seem to be advantageous when working with children and young people.

Interviews with children and young people

Simons (1982) and Lewis (1992) have identified some key difficulties when working with children and young people in interviews,

TASK 8C

Identify some of the potential difficulties you might encounter when interviewing children and young people.

....

....

....

....

....

....

but it should be remembered that some of these problems will also apply when you interview adults. Children and young people:

- can become distracted
- say what they think we want them to say
- can find it difficult to stay focused
- need language to be at the appropriate level
- may feel intimidated by an adult
- can find it difficult to articulate a response
- may find it difficult to remember
- may find it difficult to express their feelings
- may focus on one particular aspect or element, and lose the focus of the interview.

Spending some time observing the children you want to interview can be helpful, as it enables you to get to know which children work and play together and are therefore more likely to want to be together in a group or focus interview. If this is not possible, it is advisable to discuss the selected group with someone who knows them well. Brooker (2001) has noted that when the group is carefully selected the dynamics between the researcher and the respondents shift in favour of the children. This was noted by Connolly during his research into gender identity (1998) with

5- and 6-year-olds. Connolly spent several months in the school before the interviews, and had considerable familiarity with the children. He describes his role during the interview as that of 'facilitator', which was enough for the children to begin discussing the question themselves. Connolly's interventions 'were largely confined to encouraging the children to elaborate on what they had just said' (1998: 10)

Telephone interviews

It is possible to conduct any of the above types of interview by telephone. Telephone interviewing has a number of advantages. It can be cheaper to conduct telephone interviews. The researcher can select respondents from a wider geographical area and the interviews can be carried out at times convenient to the respondent. Where the research may put the researcher at risk, for example if the research involves visiting unsafe areas, the telephone interview can be used instead, to enhance safety. The response rate for telephone interviews is also higher than the response rate for questionnaires. However, there are drawbacks. It is difficult to develop a trusting relationship over the phone, and respondents may not divulge all information to the researcher. They may be suspicious of the process and may dislike sharing intimate thoughts, emotions and information over a phone. They may be concerned about confidentiality. For the researcher it is difficult to record a telephone interview. There is also a danger that the person you are speaking to isn't the person you intended to speak to. If you do need to conduct a telephone interview it is necessary to follow the advice given by Oppenheim (1992) and Miller (1995):

- Make the arrangements for the interview carefully.
- Have your questions, and follow-up questions, ready.
- Prepare in advance for the interview.
- Give your respondents time to prepare.
- Select your respondents carefully.

Questioning and probing

An important skill for the researcher to develop, whatever the interview type, is that of probing, or asking further questions designed to elicit more information from the respondent. Probing can allow the researcher to seek confirmation, clarification or elaboration from the respondent. In order to be able to probe successfully you need to have detailed knowledge about the issues linked to your research question. This knowledge is gained from your reading and study.

TASK 8D

Can you think of any questions that serve to confirm, clarify or elaborate information provided by a respondent?

....

....

....

....

....

Examples of confirmation questions include:

- So, you agree that . . .?
- Therefore, you believe that . . .?
- Do you mean . . .?

Examples of clarification questions include:

- Can you give me an example of . . .?
- What do you mean?

Examples of elaboration questions include:

- I don't understand. Can you tell me more about . . .?
- Can you give me more detail about . . .?

Bias

Researchers will have an impact upon the respondent in both positive and negative ways. Borg (1981) identifies some of these as the desire of the respondent to please the researcher, antagonism, and the desire of the researcher to seek out answers that fit with their preconceived ideas. As we noted earlier, it is easier to acknowledge that bias can occur and to exercise control in the conduct of the interview. Carrying out and assessing a pilot interview can help to alert you to your own biases.

Ethical issues

The interpersonal nature of interviews means that they have an ethical dimension that researchers should use to inform their practice. Kvale (1996) identifies the three main ethical issues as consent, confidentiality and the consequences of the interview. As we explored in Chapter 2 there are particular considerations when working with children and young people in relation to consent and confidentiality. The following checklist is helpful when considering ethics in relation to interview data:

- Has informed consent been obtained for the interviews to take place?
- Has the respondent been given information about the research project?
- Are there any potential hazards to the respondent from taking part in the interviews, and how will these be ameliorated?
- How will confidentiality and anonymity be ensured to the respondent?
- How will the interview be conducted to ensure that the respondent is not threatened in any way?
- How will the researcher verify that the data is accurate?
- Who will have access to the final research?

Conclusion

In this chapter you have been introduced to a clear conception of the interview and its purpose in research. In Chapter 9 we will look at the protocols for conducting interviews, ways of recording interviews and the design of interview schedules. Practical activities will enable you to begin the process of conducting your own research using interviews.

Chapter 9
Doing research –
successful interviewing

Introduction

In this chapter we will look at the protocols for conducting interviews, ways of recording interviews and the design of interview
schedules. Practical activities will enable you to begin the process
of conducting your own research using interviews.

If you have decided to use interviews as a method of data
collection you will need to work through the following steps in
order to ensure that the process runs smoothly.

1 Plan the interviews.
2 Design the interviews.
3 Select your respondents.
4 Organise the interviews.
5 Conduct the interviews.
6 Record the interviews.
7 Analyse the interviews.

Step 1: Planning the interviews

It is important to think through each step of the interview process in advance. You should remember that interviews are very time-consuming. You need to spend time arranging the interview, you need to construct the interview schedule, conduct the interviews, transcribe and then analyse them. For each one-hour interview that you conduct, you can reasonably expect to add three hours of planning and follow-up time. Before you begin the process it is helpful to have an idea about the topics and themes you want to explore through an interview (Task 9A).

TASK 9A

List the topics and themes you want to explore through interviews.

....

....

....

Why is an interview the most appropriate method of obtaining this information?

....

....

....

What other methods could you use?

....

....

....

Why have you decided not to use these methods?

....

....

....

Step 2: Designing the interviews

If you opt for a structured interview you need a comprehensive set of questions that you as the researcher will ask the respondent. If you have decided to use a semi-structured approach you have some flexibility, but it is still helpful to design an interview schedule to use as a prompt during the interview. Consider Cheryl's topics for discussion in a group interview with young people (Figure 9.1).

Make a list of the questions you want to ask (Task 9B). The key questions you have jotted down will be informed by your studies, your readings, your observations and discussions with others. It is important at this stage to discuss your ideas with others to see if there are any areas you have left out. Kvale (1996: 88) refers to this part of the process as thematising. It is important to thematise your interview before you decide *how* you are going to conduct the interviews.

Cheryl is designing an interview guide for her research. She wants to interview 14-year-olds about their experiences of being in college as opposed to school. The pupils attend college one day per week and are studying a vocational GCSE. Here are the questions she wants to know the answers to, which will form part of her interview schedule in semi-structured interviews with a group of 14-year-olds.

- Why did you choose to come to college?

- How did you choose the subject?

- What do you like about coming to college?

- How is college different to school?

- Do you think you will you go to college when you leave school?

Figure 9.1 Case study

TASK 9B

Make a list of the key questions you want to ask in your interviews.

....

....

....

....

....

Once you have reached this stage you can begin to design the interview schedule. You will need to think carefully about the structure of the interview. Do some questions fit logically together? Do some questions follow on from preceding ones? It is helpful for a respondent to have questions that are linked together rather than face a volley of questions that appear to be asked randomly. You should also think about the nature of response that your respondent will give. Will it be a Yes/No answer, or one which requires a fuller verbal response? Kerlinger (1970) has identified three distinct types of question we can use in an interview. First there are those questions requiring an either/or response. These are called *fixed alternative* questions. The advantage of a fixed alternative question is that you can easily analyse the responses you obtain. However, these questions can be quite irritating to the respondent, particularly if you use too many of them. The second type of question we can use is an *open ended* question. These allow the respondent to provide as much or as little information as they choose. The third type of question is a *scale* question. These require the respondent to rank their response to a statement.

The golden rule with questions is to make them clear and easy to understand. As we saw with questionnaires, there is no place for overly technical language or poorly worded questions. A mixture of the question types can add variety to the interview. What is most important is that you select the most appropriate question format to meet your research needs.

TASK 9C

Look at the following questions. Decide which type of question each one is.

Question: What type of music do you listen to?

Type: ....

Question: Have you visited the Eiffel Tower?

Type: ....

Question: Read the following statement: *The National Curriculum stifles creativity*.

Please circle your response.

Do you:

Agree strongly	Agree	Neither agree nor disagree	Disagree	Disagree strongly

Type: ....

Having identified the variety of questions we can use in an interview we now need to think about the nature of the question. In Chapter 4 we explored the Morgan and Saxton (1991) definition of questions that stimulate thinking:

- questions that draw upon knowledge (remembering)
- questions that test comprehension (understanding)
- questions that require application (solving)
- questions that encourage analysis (reasoning)
- questions that invite synthesis (creating)
- questions that promote evaluation (judging).

TASK 9D

Write an example related to your own research of the three question types.

Fixed alternative question:

....

....

....

Open ended question:

....

....

....

Scale question:

....

....

....

TASK 9E

Look at your questions in Task 9D. Which of the Morgan and Saxton question classifications have you used?

....

....

....

Can you write additional questions linked to the classifications you have not used that are related to your research?

....

....

....

You should now be in a position where you have designed your interview schedule and piloted it with an appropriate person or group. You now need to think about who you will interview.

Step 3: Selecting your respondents

You should ensure that the people you select to interview will generate the data you require. If your research is looking at the experiences of young Asian girls it would be inappropriate to interview Afro-Caribbean girls, for example. Your sample should also be representative, to ensure that your data is not skewed. Consider the case study in Figure 9.2.

Step 4: Organising the interviews

You need to follow a strict etiquette when interviewing. You should always try to make personal contact with the person you want to interview. This enables you to explain the purpose of your research and to gain their consent to participate. You should fix a date and time for the interview and confirm this in writing. It is also helpful if you can indicate how long the interview will last. A sample contact letter is provided in Figure 9.3.

You should also make sure that you have obtained the necessary permissions from respondents, particularly if your interviews will involve children or young people.

Step 5: Conducting the interviews

On the day of the interview you should ensure that you know exactly where you are going and arrive in plenty of time. You will need to set up the interview room when you arrive. A table can be helpful if you are using recording equipment. It is also helpful to have a firm surface to write your own notes on. However, it is best to avoid an 'over the table' encounter when interviewing as this

Angie has decided to interview TAs about their self-esteem as part of her research into the professionalism of TAs. She has identified eight TAs to interview from a variety of schools.

When she analyses her interviews she discovers that the TAs have very low self-esteem and can be very self-deprecating about the work they do. Angie doesn't understand this, as the TAs she works with are self-confident.

When she looks at the interviews again she realises that the people she interviewed all work in schools with specific issues. Two of the schools have had poor OFSTED reports, three are in areas of high deprivation and have low attainment in national tests, one school has had several headteachers in a short space of time and one is undergoing an amalgamation which may result in job losses. Only one of the schools in her sample would be described as 'ordinary'.

Upon reflection, Angie realises that she should have taken greater care to choose a range of schools, as the working environment can affect self-esteem.

Figure 9.2 Case study

can be intimidating for the respondent. They are there to help you in your research, not apply for a job! Field and Morse (1989) identify a number of steps the researcher can take to ensure that the interview proceeds smoothly. These include preventing interruptions during the interview. This can be done by putting a polite notice on the door. Similarly, it is important to minimise distractions. An interview will not proceed smoothly if the respondent is visually or aurally distracted. The researcher should remain focused and not jump from one topic to another, nor should they summarise what the respondent is saying. Finally, it is important to handle sensitive matters with respondents carefully.

When your respondent arrives for the interview you should introduce yourself and clearly explain the purpose of your research and

Anywhere College
Somewhere Rd
Anyplace
AB1 2CD

9 January 2006

Dear Claire

Title of Project: The role of play in Y2 in raising standards in numeracy

Thank you for agreeing to take part in the above research project. As a participant in this study, you will be interviewed about your experiences of using play in year 2.

The interview will take place at **Common Rd School** in the Medical Room on **Monday February 10th 2006 at 2pm. The interview should last for approximately 1 hr.**

Participation in this study is voluntary, and will take approximately one hour of your time. There are no personal benefits to participation, however you will receive a copy of the final report when it is published. You may decline to answer any questions presented during the study if you so wish. Further, you may decide to withdraw from this study at any time. All information you provide is completely confidential and your name will not be included, or in any other way associated, with the data collected in the study. Furthermore, because the interest of this study is in the average responses of all participants, you will not be identified individually in any way in any written reports of this research. Data collected during this study will be retained indefinitely, in a locked office to which only the lead researcher has access. There are no known or anticipated risks associated with participation in this study.

If you have any comments or concerns resulting from your participation in this study, please contact me directly on 07654 987654.

Yours sincerely

Jenny

Jenny Foster

Figure 9.3 Sample interview consent letter

TASK 9F

Where will your interviews take place?

....

....

What special arrangements will you need to make before the day of the interview?

....

....

....

....

---

what format the interview will take. If you are intending to record the interview you should ask the respondent's permission. Never record an interview without obtaining consent to do so. It is helpful to ask your respondent to sign a consent form at the beginning of the interview. A sample consent form is provided in Figure 9.4.

At the end of the interview you should thank your respondent and confirm the arrangements for follow-up. It is customary to send the participants in your research a copy of the final report.

Step 6: Recording the interviews

An interview that lasts for one hour will generate a substantial amount of information. If the questions you have selected for the interview are scale or fixed alternative, recording the responses will be straightforward. You can simply annotate a copy of the interview schedule and note the respondent's answers. However, open-ended questions need detailed notes in order to preserve the content of the interview. Many researchers like to audio record the interview to ensure that all data is preserved. It is helpful to transcribe each interview but this is a lengthy process. Whichever

---

Title of Project: The role of play in Y2 in raising standards in numeracy

CONSENT FORM

I agree to participate in a study being conducted by Jenny Foster. I have made this decision based on the information I have received and I have had the opportunity to receive any additional details I wanted about the study. I understand that I may withdraw this consent at any time. I understand that the interview will be tape-recorded.

Name of respondent: ....

Signature: ....

Date: ....

Name of researcher: ....

Signature: ....

Date: ....

Figure 9.4 Sample consent form

method you choose the aim is to ensure that you have an accurate record of what the respondent said.

If you choose to audio record an interview you should bear the following points in mind. Ensure that your recording equipment works and has fully charged batteries. It is helpful to carry spares just in case! Position the microphone so that it will record each voice evenly and clearly. It is a good idea to test the equipment with the respondent to make sure that it is working correctly. Label your audio tapes as you work. Audio tapes vary in length, with some lasting for only 30 minutes. You will use multiple tapes if you are interviewing several people and it is easy to get them muddled up. At the start of each interview ask the respondent to state their name for the tape. This way, if there is a mix-up in your

---

TASK 9G

What potential problems are there when audio recording an interview?

....
....
....
....
....

---

labelling it will be easy to resolve. Practise changing the tape quickly. With short audio tapes you do not want to stop your respondent in the middle of a sentence so that you can swap the tape over. With practice this can be done quickly and unobtrusively and little data is lost. After the interview make sure that you store the tapes somewhere secure and begin the process of transcription. It is much easier to work with one interview at a time rather than face transcribing several interviews in one go.

Video recording can be used during interviews and can capture gestures and aspects of non-verbal communication that a tape recording can miss. However, the equipment is obtrusive and may make the respondent uncomfortable.

TASK 9H

What method will you use to record your interviews? Justify your response.

....
....
....
....
....

During the interview the researcher has a considerable amount of responsibility. Cohen *et al.* (2000: 279) identify the following as specific responsibilities. The researcher must ensure that the cognitive element of the interview is appropriate. This comes from knowing the subject in depth and being able to probe the respondents effectively. The researcher has a responsibility for the ethical conduct of the interview. The researcher must address the interpersonal, interactional, communicative and emotional aspects of the interview. They must be active listeners and pay attention to body language. Verbal communication should be considered carefully. It may be appropriate to use colloquialisms to put the respondent at ease during an interview. The researcher must ensure that the dynamics of the interview are maintained. This means keeping the conversation flowing. Whyte (1982) identified a six-point scale of researcher 'directiveness':

1   Researcher makes encouraging noises – um, aha, uh uh etc.
2   Researcher reflects on remarks made by respondent.
3   Researcher probes last comment by the respondent.
4   Researcher probes an idea that precedes the last remark made by the respondent.
5   Researcher probes an idea expressed earlier in the interview.
6   Researcher introduces a new topic.

Whyte argues that skilful researchers will use these as appropriate during an interview. Kvale (1996: 145) argues that the ideal interview has distinct 'quality criteria' which are summarised below:

- In the interview the dominant voice is that of the respondent – short questions with long responses are the ideal.
- The interview contains rich, relevant and specific answers.
- The researcher follows up, clarifies, verifies and probes points made by the respondent throughout the interview.
- The interview can be easily understood – it has a conversational feel and tells the story of the respondent's experience.

Step 7: Analysing the interviews

After an interview you need to analyse the data you have collected. This involves listening to the audio tapes, reading the transcripts and beginning the process of making sense. This process is explored in Chapter 11.

Conclusion

In this chapter you have worked through each of the steps necessary to conduct an interview. In Chapter 11 you will look at the process of analysing your data. In Chapters 4–9 you have been introduced to the three key methods of gathering information in a research project. These methods are widely used by researchers in a variety of settings and are well-documented. If you wish to learn more about alternative methods of gathering data the book by Cohen *et al.* (2000) will provide you with a thorough overview.

In Chapter 10 we look at an alternative form of conducting research that closely links the researcher and the context in which they work. This is known as action research.

Chapter 10
Looking at research –
action research

Introduction

In this chapter we will look at a method of conducting research in education that clearly links the act of research with the context in which the research is carried out, with the intention of developing practice within that context. It will begin with an overview of what action research is, and the different forms it can take. A discussion of the tools available to the researcher for action research and the specific role that the researcher takes will be outlined, as will the ethical considerations you must take into account if you choose this method of research.

What is action research?

> Action research is simply a form of self-reflective enquiry undertaken by participants in social situations in order to improve the rationality and justice of their own practices, their understanding of these practices, and the situations in which the practices are carried out.
>
> (Carr and Kemmis 1986: 162)

Action research is firmly located in the hands of the practitioner, and as a way of working it is very close to the notion of reflective practice developed by Schön (1983). He argued that 'reflection' was at the centre of an understanding of what professionals do. Usher *et al.* claim that Schön looks to an alternative epistemology of practice 'in which the knowledge inherent in practice is to be understood as artful doing' (Usher *et al.* 1997: 143). The concepts of reflection-in-action, and reflection-on-action were central to Schön's theory. Reflection in action can be described as 'thinking on your feet'. It involves looking to our experiences, connecting these with our feelings and trying to understand which theoretical frameworks we are using to make sense of the experience. We actively and continuously build new understandings to inform our actions in the situation that is unfolding. More importantly, the practitioner carries out small experiments that serve to generate a new understanding of the situation and effect a positive change (Schön 1983: 68). The practitioner tests out 'theories', which in turn lead to new actions. Drawing upon what has gone before, the practitioner thinks carefully about the way in which they will change what they do, which often involves the rejection of established ideas and ways of doing things.

Reflection-on-action, in contrast, is done after the event has taken place. We can reflect on action in many ways – writing up the event in a journal, discussing the event with a colleague, etc. In doing so we spend time exploring why we acted as we did, what was happening and why. This enables us to develop further questions and ideas about our activities and practice. Schön argued that practitioners draw upon a collection of images, ideas, examples and actions that help them to make sense of an event. This is their 'repertoire' and is central to reflective thought, as they later draw upon the repertoire in making sense of the event:

> When a practitioner makes sense of a situation he perceives to be unique, he sees it as something already present in his repertoire . . . It is . . . to see the unfamiliar, unique situation as both similar to and different from the familiar one, without at first being able to say similar or different with

> respect to what. The familiar situation functions as a pre-
> cedent, or a metaphor, or . . . an exemplar for the unfamiliar
> one.
>
> (Schön 1983: 138)

When a practitioner is reflecting upon an event and being influenced by their repertoire they are also drawing upon routines and
memory, which enables them to build theories and responses that
fit the new situation. They might not have a full understanding of
the event but they can engage with the situation.

There are many definitions in the literature of reflection. Most,
however, agree that it is an active, conscious process. Reflection
begins when a practitioner encounters some problematic aspect of
practice and attempts to make sense of it. Dewey (1933) defined
reflection as the active, persistent and careful consideration of any
knowledge in the light of the grounds that support it and the further
conclusions to which it leads. Dewey worked as an educationalist
and developed his concept of reflective practice and reflection
through experiential learning theories. Boud *et al.* (1985) take a
different perspective and define reflection as the generic term for
intellectual activities practitioners engage in to explore their experiences with the aim of creating new understanding. Boud *et al.*
view reflection from the learner's point of view. They emphasise
the relationship of the reflective process and the learning experience. Reid (1993) noted that reflection was an active process rather
than passive thinking. Reflection is a process of reviewing practice
in order to describe, analyse, evaluate and inform learning about
practice. Kemmis (1985) argues that reflection is a positive,
active process that reviews, analyses and evaluates experiences,
draws on theoretical concepts or previous learning and provides an
action plan for future experiences. Reflection enables the practitioner to assess, understand and learn through their experiences. It
is a highly personal process that usually results in some change for
the individual in their perspective of a situation or creates new
learning for the individual. The outcome of reflection as identified
by Mezirow (1981) is learning.

TASK 10A

Identify the advantages of action research.

....

....

....

Why is action research an effective tool in educational contexts?

....

....

....

....

Action research methodology offers a systematic approach to introducing innovations in education. It does this by putting the practitioner in the dual role of producer of educational knowledge and user of that knowledge. It is a way of producing knowledge about education and a powerful way of improving educational practice. It connects theory and practice together. Action research has a number of distinctive features (Zuber-Skerritt 1982). Action research is critical collaborative enquiry that is engaged in by reflective practitioners. These practitioners are accountable to public enquiry – they must share their results. They must be self-evaluative in their practice, and willing to engage in participative problem-solving and continuing professional development. According to this view, action research is critical because practitioners not only look for ways to improve their practice within the various constraints of the situation in which they are working, but they also act as critical change agents.

Forms of action research

Kurt Lewin is credited as the person who coined the term 'action research'. He argued that 'research that produces nothing but books will not suffice' (Lewin 1946, reproduced in Lewin 1948: 202–3).

His approach involves a continuing spiral of steps, 'each of which is composed of a circle of planning, action and fact-finding about the result of the action' (ibid. 206). The basic cycle involves the following:

1   Identifying a problem/general idea/initial idea.
2   Fact finding.
3   Planning.
4   Taking initial action.
5   Evaluating the outcomes of the action.
6   Amending the plan.
7   Taking second action.

First the practitioner examines their idea carefully in the light of the means available. Frequently more fact-finding about the situation is required. If this first period of planning is successful, two items emerge: an overall plan of how to reach the objective and a decision about the first step of action. Usually this planning process leads to a modification of the initial idea (ibid. 205). The practitioner then undertakes 'a circle of planning, executing, and reconnaissance or fact finding for the purpose of evaluating the results of the second step, and preparing the rational basis for planning the third step, and for perhaps modifying again the overall plan' (ibid. 206). This approach to research is oriented to problem-solving in social and organisational settings.

Two distinguishing characteristics of action research are the empowerment given to all participants and the central importance of communication. Participants construct meaning from the data and there are no hidden controls or pre-emption of direction by the researcher. All participants contribute to the selection of intervention strategies. In an education context this might include the researchers, the teachers and the students. Kemmis and McTaggart argue that communication between all participants should be of paramount importance:

> Since action research looks at a problem from the point of view of those involved it can only be validated in

unconstrained dialogue with them . . . Since action research
involves unconstrained dialogue between 'researcher'
(whether he be an outsider or teacher/researcher) and the participants, there must be free information flow between them.
Kemmis and McTaggart 1990:122)

A variety of forms of action research have evolved (Carr and
Kemmis 1986). All adopt a methodical approach embracing
problem identification, action planning, implementation, evaluation
and reflection. The insights gained from the initial cycle feed into
the planning of the second cycle, for which the action plan is modi-
fied and the research process repeated (see Figure 10.1).

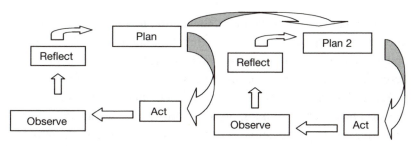

Figure 10.1 The action research cycle

Kolb (1984) extended this model to offer a conception of the
action research cycle as a learning process, whereby people learn
and create knowledge by critically reflecting upon their own actions
and experiences, forming abstract concepts, and testing the implications of these concepts in new situations. Practitioners can create
their own knowledge and understanding of a situation and act upon
it, thereby improving practice and advancing knowledge in the field.
His model suggests that there are four stages, which follow from
each other (see Figure 10.2).

Concrete experience is followed by reflection on that experience on a personal basis. This is then followed by the creation of
general rules to describe the experience, or the application of known
theories to it (abstract conceptualisation). Ways of modifying the
next occurrence of the experience (active experimentation) lead in
turn to the next concrete experience.

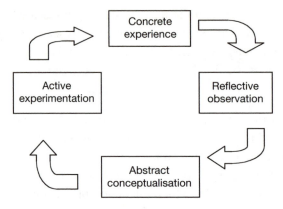

Figure10.2 Kolb's learning cycle

Stringer (1999) has identified that action research works through three basic phases. Phase one is the looking phase. We build a picture and gather information. When evaluating we define and describe the problem to be investigated and the context in which it is set. The actions of all of the participants are described. The second phase is the thinking phase. In this phase we analyse, interpret and explain the situation. We reflect on what participants have been doing. We look at areas of success and any deficiencies, issues or problems. The final phase is the action phase when issues and problems are resolved. In evaluation we judge the worth, effectiveness, appropriateness, and outcomes of those activities. We act to formulate solutions to any problems (Stringer 1999: 18, 43–4, 160).

Another tradition within action research is to see it used widely within the social welfare field as 'the systematic collection of information that is designed to bring about social change' (Bogdan and Biklen 1982: 223). Bogdan and Biklen argue that practitioners collect evidence or data to expose unjust practices or environmental dangers and recommend actions for change. The practitioner is actively involved in the cause for which the research is conducted. Such a commitment is a necessary part of being a practitioner.

Action research is different from what we do as practitioners. It is not the usual thinking that we do in relation to our work, because it is more systematic and collaborative in collecting

TASK 10B

Can you identify any potential problems with the concept of action research?

....

....

....

....

....

evidence that will then be subject to group reflection. It is more than simply problem solving as action research often means that problems are generated from the desire to make things better. Action researchers are motivated by a desire to understand and effect changes. As a result, this form of research is not done to people but actively involves them and it does not follow any proscribed methods. The advantages of this model are that it can be empowering and increase professionalism. Some argue that it can be the main tool of professional development (Nixon 1981, Winter 1996). It is a form of workplace-based learning which entails learning about the workplace but also learning within it.

Action research suffered a decline in favour during the 1960s because it was linked to political activism (Stringer 1999: 9). There have been several criticisms of action research. Some argue that it is not emancipatory (Kemmis 1997) and ignores the subtle power relations inherent in human experience. In some of the earlier work on action research (Lewin and Grabbe 1945) there was a tension between providing a rational basis for change through research, and the recognition that individuals are constrained in their ability to change by their cultural and social perceptions and the social structures that they inhabit. Having knowledge does not automatically mean that change will occur. We need to pay attention to the '"matrix of cultural and psychic forces" through which the subject is constituted' (Winter 1987: 48). Others argue that the emphasis on groups of people undermines the work of the single researcher and may privilege some groups over others (Kemmis and McTaggart 1992). Implicit in the model is the idea that group consensus will emerge, which may not always be the case. Just why it must be collective is open to question (Webb 1996). That action research is based upon reflective practice may be problematic. For example, Schön's distinction between reflection in and on action is not as straightforward as it first appears. Eraut (1994) argues that 'when time is extremely short, decisions have to be rapid and the scope for reflection is extremely limited' (1994: 145). To argue that there is a difference in types of reflection may be problematic as a result. However, as Bogdan and Biklen (1982: 223) argue, research is a frame of mind – 'a perspective that people take toward objects and activities'. If the collection of information is systematic, and interpretations made have a proper regard for satisfying truth claims, then many of the criticisms levelled at action research disappear. The problem of such models is that action research becomes little more than a procedure. McTaggart (1996: 248) argues that to think that following the action research spiral constitutes 'doing action research' is fallacious. He continues, 'Action research is not a "method" or a "procedure" for research but a series of commitments to observe and problematize through practice a series of principles for conducting social enquiry'. The notion of a spiral or cycle may be a useful teaching device but there is a danger that it becomes the template for practice (McTaggart 1996: 249).

Action research tools

Action Research is a holistic approach to problem solving, rather than a single method for collecting and analysing data. Several different research tools can be used as the research is carried out.

Most of the methods selected are those used in qualitative research, which is not surprising given the importance of the construction of meaning within action research. Methods used might include keeping a research journal, document analysis, observation, questionnaires and interviews. A research method that has been designed specifically to meet the needs of this approach is the search

---

TASK 10C

What methods do you think someone conducting action research in a school setting might use?

....

....

....

....

....

---

conference. This was developed by Trist in 1959. Searching is carried out in groups that are composed of the relevant stakeholders. The group meets exclusively to discuss the idea or problem. Meeting content is contributed entirely by the members of the group. The researcher acts as a facilitator. Only when all of the ideas have been discussed does the group move towards formulating a plan of action.

Kemmis and McTaggart (1992: 25–7) have provided a helpful checklist for researchers contemplating the use of action research.

- Get an action research group together – this might be a natural grouping in your workplace, or you may wish to invite other people to participate who you don't normally work with to gain a differing perspective.
- Be organised – set a timeline for the research.
- Arrange a way to monitor progress against the timeline.
- Ensure that you regularly report the outcomes of each stage of the research as widely as possible.
- Don't expect to change everything – action research can be a long, slow process.
- Ensure that you remain open to changing everything – this includes the way you think about things and the language you use.
- Write up the outcomes of the research and be explicit about what you have achieved.

- Throughout the research keep asking yourself what you are achieving – are you changing anything?

Cohen *et al.* (2000: 237) argue that action research is 'a blend of practical and theoretical concerns, it is both action and research'.

The role of the action researcher

The researcher's role within the organisation is to implement the action research method in such a way that all participants contribute to a mutually agreeable process with a clear outcome, with the process of action research often being maintained by the organisation after the initial impetus of the researcher. In order to do this the researcher needs to adopt many different roles.

You may need to adopt the role of research planner in the initial stages before the participants adopt the process for themselves. You may need to be a leader of the group or a facilitator. It could be that your role is to challenge preconceived ideas about the way in which a problem should be solved, placing you in the position of acting as a catalyst for change. You will need to adopt a variety of communication roles – the listener, the reporter, the teacher, etc. You will also need to adopt the roles that accompany the research method you adopt – you may be an interviewer or an observer.

TASK 10D

What roles do you think you would need to adopt if you conducted action research?

....

....

....

....

....

....

Ethical considerations

Action research is carried out in the real world and involves close and open communication with a variety of participants. Ethical considerations should guide the actions of the researcher. Winter (1996) identifies a number of principles. The relevant persons, committees and authorities should be consulted and the principles guiding the research accepted in advance by everyone participating in the research. All participants must be allowed to influence the research. This means that decisions about the research should be made collectively. The wishes of those who do not want to participate must be respected. The development of the work must remain visible and open to suggestions from others. Permission must be obtained before making observations or examining documents produced for other purposes. Descriptions of others' work and points of view must be negotiated with those concerned before being published. The researcher must accept responsibility for maintaining confidentiality (Winter 1996).

Conclusion

In this chapter we have looked at action research as a possible method for conducting research in education. We have identified that a key advantage of this form of research is that it clearly links the act of research with the context in which the research is carried out. It is also emancipatory and has the intention of developing practice within that context, which makes it an attractive form of research for practitioners to engage in. We have also, however, noted the limitations, and that action research should not be viewed as the employed researcher's automatic research tool.

Chapter 11
Analysing research data

Introduction

In this chapter we will look at how researchers begin to make sense of all of the information they have collected through their interviews, observations and questionnaires. You will carry out practical activities based around the data you have collected that will help you to begin the process of identifying what you have found out during your research.

When we analyse our data we are looking for patterns, groupings, similarities and differences. This is what you will write about – what you will analyse. You may already have ideas about what you think the data will tell you, but you need to be open to the unexpected. It is important not to let your preconceived ideas about the subject inform your interpretation of the data. When researchers need to sum up the characteristics or actions of a group they use statistics. In this chapter you will be introduced to some basic statistical tools that will help you analyse and present your data.

Interpreting and presenting data from questionnaires

In previous chapters we looked at the use of questionnaires and interviews, and how to construct them. This means that you will have a series of questions that you can work with in this chapter. We have identified a variety of question types. These question types can be interpreted using various strategies.

Responses to choice questions, where the respondent chooses their response from a list, are the easiest to present, particularly when the list is simple. Figure 11.1 demonstrates a simple list question.

To present the response to this question we need to create a summary sheet to count up the number of responses for each item in the list. A tally sheet can be used to do this. Imagine that you sent out 15 questionnaires. Figure 11.2 shows the response you might have obtained to the question.

We now know the following facts:

- All of the teaching assistants who completed the question-naire hold a qualification above Level 2.
- Most of the teaching assistants who completed the questionnaire hold a Level 3 qualification.
- Only one of the teaching assistants who completed the questionnaire has completed a BA degree.

Q6 What is your highest level of teaching assistant qualification?
(*Please tick*)

NVQ Level 2	☐
NVQ Level 3	☐
Foundation degree	☐
BA degree	☐

Figure 11.1 List question

Question 6
Highest level of teaching assistant qualification

NVQ level 2	NVQ level 3	Foundation degree	BA degree
	ЖІ ЖІ	ІІІІ	І
0	10	4	1

Figure 11.2 Sample tally sheet

- Ten people hold a Level 3 qualification.
- Four people hold a foundation degree.

We can now choose to present this information to our reader in a table or on a bar chart. To show the responses to Q6 as a table you need to turn the question into a statement. This is usually the title of the table. Figure 11.3 demonstrates how we can then show how many people who completed the questionnaire fit into each category.

We number the tables according to the chapter they are in. So in our example the table has been put into Chapter 5 or part 5 of the final report. It is the first table in that chapter so it has been identified as Table 5.1. Using a simple numbering system such as this makes it clear for the reader.

NVQ level 2	NVQ level 3	Foundation degree	BA degree
0	10	4	1

TABLE 5.1 Teaching assistants' qualifications

Figure 11.3 Teaching assistants' qualifications

A bar chart is a way of presenting data that allows similar items in a group to be compared. The frequency of each item of data is illustrated by the length of the bars. To show the responses to question 6 as a bar chart you need to put the variable category (type of qualification) along the horizontal axis and the frequency (number of people) on the vertical axis. This is demonstrated in Figure 11.4.

You now need to decide on a frequency interval. For example, you could mark the vertical axis in intervals of 1. But this would make the axis very large. Large-scale population studies count in millions! It is easier to group in 5s or 10s if you have large numbers of responses to show. If you are working with 20 or less responses, grouping in 2s is appropriate. This is demonstrated in Figure 11.5. The frequency bars are equally spaced on the vertical axis.

We can now add columns to show the number of responses in each category (Figure 11.6). Note that the bars on the horizontal axis are the same width. You can use colour or shading to make them easier to read and they must be labelled. In Figure 11.6 we have called the bar chart Figure 5.1 rather than use the table prefix.

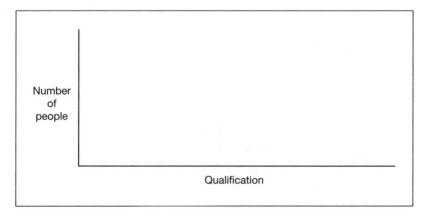

Figure 11.4 Structure of a bar chart

You may want to show your information as a percentage. What percentage of the people who completed the questionnaire have a qualification above Level 3?

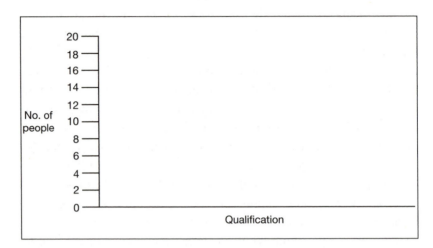

Figure 11.5 A bar chart showing frequency intervals

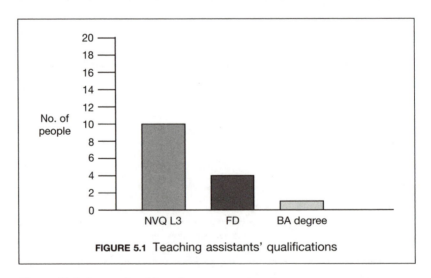

FIGURE 5.1 Teaching assistants' qualifications

Figure 11.6 A completed bar chart

Calculating percentages

To calculate a percentage, use this formula:

$$\text{(specific amount} \div \text{total)} \times 100 = \text{percentage}$$

Let's look at how this works. Imagine that you have interviewed 14 people about their favourite colour:

    7 prefer red
    3 prefer blue
    4 prefer green

To calculate the percentage who like each colour we use the formula as follows:

Red:

$$(7 \text{ (people who chose red)} \div 14 \text{ (total number of people))} \times 100 = \%$$
$$(7 \div 14) \times 100$$
$$0.5 \times 100$$
$$= 50\%$$

Blue:

$$(3 \text{ (people who chose blue)} \div 14 \text{ (total number of people))} \times 100 = \%$$
$$(3 \div 14) \times 100$$
$$0.21 \times 100$$
$$= 21\%$$

Green:

$$(4 \text{ (people who chose green)} \div 14 \text{ (total number of people))} \times 100 = \%$$
$$(4 \div 14) \times 100$$
$$0.29 \times 100$$
$$= 29\%$$

Red = 50%   Blue = 21%   Green = 29%

The total must equal 100%.

TASK 11A

Use the data in the previous example (Figure 11.2) to calculate the percentage of teaching assistants with each qualification.

....
....
....
....
....
....
....
....

Answers to 11A

Teaching assistants with level 3

(10 (people with NVQ level 3) ÷ 15 (total number of people)) × 100 = %

(10 ÷ 15) × 100

0.67 × 100

= 67%

Teaching assistants with a foundation degree

(4 (people with foundation degree) ÷ 15 (total number of people)) × 100 = %

(4 ÷ 15) × 100

0.27 × 100

= 27%

Teaching assistants with a BA degree

(1 (person with BA degree) ÷ 15 (total number of people)) × 100 = %

(1 ÷ 15) × 100

0.06 × 100

= 6%

Remember when using figures to round up and down as necessary. Calculating the percentage is helpful when you come to write your analysis. To our list of facts about question 6 we could now add the following statements.

- 27 per cent of those who completed the questionnaire hold a foundation degree.
- Only 6 per cent of those who completed the questionnaire hold a BA degree.
- Therefore 94 per cent hold a qualification below BA degree level.
- The majority 67 per cent hold an NVQ Level 3 qualification.
- Only 33 per cent have a qualification higher than Level 3.

Pie charts

You can visually represent your data using a pie chart. A pie chart is based upon a circle. The total area of the circle represents 100 per cent of the information, and is divided into segments, each of which represents a category of information. Therefore, they are used to compare different parts of the same whole. To draw a pie chart we need to represent each part of the data as a proportion of 360, because there are 360 degrees in a circle. Consider the following example: 270 children were asked to identify their favourite food from a list. The responses are shown in Figure 11.7.

We use the following formula to work out the degrees of the total circle we will use for each response:

(number of responses ÷ total number) × 360 = degrees of the
whole circle

For example, if 55 children chose crisps out of 270 responses then we will represent this on the circle as:

(55 ÷ 270) × 360 = 73 degrees

The rest of the calculations can be found in Figure 11.8.

Favourite food	Number of children
Chips	140
Burger	70
Crisps	55
Chocolate	5
Total number	270

Figure 11.7 Responses to 'favourite food' question

We draw this information up using a protractor and compass, and end up with the data represented as in Figure 11.9. A pie chart can be awkward to draw using a protractor and compass, but if you have access to a computer programme such as Microsoft Excel you will find the process easier. Figure 11.10 gives the correct answers to the calculations, and Figure 11.11. demonstrates how this is then presented as a pie chart.

We can use the techniques introduced above to analyse a range of question types – not just list questions. If your question is a rank order or scale question, you can apply the techniques to the different categories.

TASK 11B

Using the data in Figure 11.2 and your responses to Task 11A draw a pie chart to represent the data.

Favourite food	Number of children	Calculation	Degrees of the circle
Chips	140	(140 ÷ 270) × 360 = 187	187
Burger	70	(70 ÷ 270) × 360 = 93	93
Crisps	55	(55 ÷ 270) × 360 = 73	73
Chocolate	5	(5 ÷ 270) × 360 = 7	7
Total number	270		360

Figure 11.8 Completed pie chart calculations

Children's preferred food

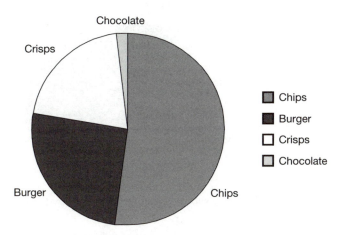

Figure 11.9 Chart showing children's preferred food

You may have conducted a research project where you will have two sets of information that you want to compare. For example, you may have looked at whether Year 6 SATs scores are linked to an assessment test carried out in the school at the start of Year 6, to discover whether the assessment test can be used to predict attainment in the Year 6 SAT. Let us suppose that you obtained the data in Figure 11.12.

TA highest qualification	Number of responses	Calculation	Degrees of the circle
NVQ Level 2	0	(0 ÷ 15) × 360 = 0	0
NVQ Level 3	10	(10 ÷ 15) × 360 = 240	240
Foundation degree	4	(4 ÷ 15) × 360 = 96	96
BA degree	1	(1 ÷ 150) × 360 = 24	24
Total number	15		360

Figure 11.10 Answers to the calculation

Qualifications of teaching assistants

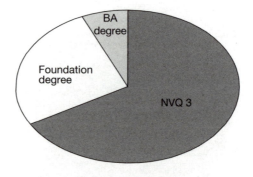

Figure 11.11 Pie chart showing qualifications held by teaching assistants

What you will notice is that in all cases the pupils' scores are equal. It is unlikely that this would happen. We are using this example to illustrate the fact that there is a *positive correlation* between the two sets of data. The higher the assessment test score, the higher the SAT test score. Figure 11.13 demonstrates what happens when this is plotted on a graph.

The table in Figure 11.14 shows a *negative correlation*. The lower the assessment score, the higher the SAT score. It would be highly unusual to find that assessment data did not have positive

Pupil	Assessment test score	SAT test score
A	70	70
B	75	75
C	80	80
D	85	85
E	90	90
F	95	95
G	100	100

Figure 11.12 Year 6 assessment test and SAT scores

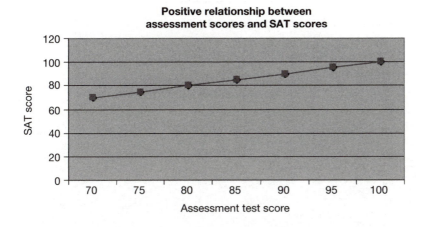

Figure 11.13 A graph demonstrating a positive correlation between data

relationship with Year 6 SATs data. Figure 11.15 is telling us that a child with a low assessment test score is going to achieve a high SAT score.

It is more likely that the data you collect will not correlate perfectly. Figure 11.16 contains more realistic data. This produces

Pupil	Assessment test score	SAT test score
G	70	100
H	75	95
I	80	90
J	85	85
K	90	80
L	95	75
M	100	70

Figure 11.14 Data with a negative correlation

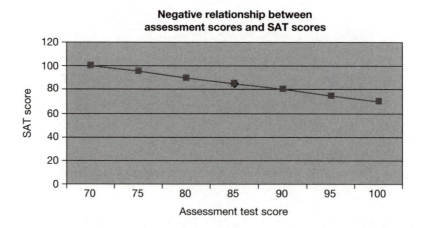

Figure 11.15 A graph demonstrating a negative correlation between data

a more random pattern on the graph (Figure 11.17). It is still possible to group items together, or to note where there are isolated items that warrant further investigation.

There are complex calculations for deriving correlation coefficients (the accuracy of the correlation), and programs such as the Statistical Package for the Social Science (SPSS) enable researchers to undertake this level of analysis. However, it is unlikely that you will be required to do so as part of a small-scale research project.

TASK 11C

Using your own research data begin the process of statistical analysis. Consider:

....
....
....

Which data will you present as a bar chart?

....
....
....

Which data will be presented in tables?

....
....
....

Which data will be presented as a pie chart?

....
....
....

How will you present data if you don't use the above methods?

....
....
....

Pupil	Assessment test score	SAT test score
G	72	85
H	76	78
I	82	81
J	85	85
K	71	79
L	68	80
M	92	95

Figure 11.16 A typical data set with no clear correlation

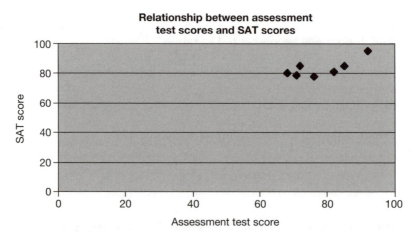

Figure 11.17 A graph demonstrating no clear correlation between data

Data from interviews and open questions

A questionnaire may contain responses to open questions. We analyse these in a similar way to responses obtained in interviews. The first stage is to record all of the responses you have obtained to the open question. You then need to begin to group the responses to identify any similarities or recurring themes. It may be that you have identified some themes already and these might be a useful starting point for organising your data. You will find it helpful to adopt a systematic approach to the analysis of your data. It is easier to analyse one interview at a time and record items on a summary sheet than to work with multiple questionnaire returns.

When we analyse interview data or data provided in response to open questions, the task becomes interpretive. The researcher needs to look at what the participants have said and make sense of it in relation to the research question. There are several stages in this analysis. The first is to look at the data and identify units of meaning. Consider the example in Task 11D.

The researcher has asked whether behaviour is a problem in the school. Units of meaning we can generate are highlighted in Figure 11.18 which highlights the key statements.

Researcher: Is pupil behaviour a problem in the school?

Participant: I think right across the spectrum we've got problems, not just school, outside in the street, everywhere, behaviour is a problem at the moment in society and I think there is a lack of respect for authority, and there's also er . . . this, erm . . . this attitude of er . . . some of these students just don't want to be here, don't want to do it or don't want to do it when they feel like it, and I think that attitude's got to be changed and I think it's going to be a hard job; and I think it's not just us who're suffering, but that has definitely been a problem here, with the behaviour, it, it, it's. . . . I wouldn't say we've got a major behaviour problem, but what I would say is that we've got a major problem with attitude that we've got to change, we've got to start bringing respect back into the school, and we've got to start bringing in a little bit of er . . . discipline back.

Figure 11.18 Key statement identification

TASK 11D

Look at this extract from a research interview. The researcher is tying to find out if behaviour policies impact upon the way staff manage pupils.

Researcher: Is pupil behaviour a problem in the school?

Participant: I think right across the spectrum we've got problems, not just school, outside in the street, everywhere, behaviour is a problem at the moment in society and I think there is a lack of respect for authority, and there's also er. . . this, erm. . . this attitude of er. . . some of these students just don't want to be here, don't want to do it or don't want to do it when they feel like it, and I think that attitude's got to be changed and I think it's going to be a hard job; and I think it's not just us who're suffering, but that has definitely been a problem here, with the behaviour, it, it, it's . . . I wouldn't say we've got a major behaviour problem, but what I would say is that we've got a major problem with attitude that we've got to change, we've got to start bringing respect back into the school, and we've got to start bringing in a little bit of er. . . discipline back.

What units of meaning can you derive from it?

....

....

....

....

....

....

....

....

....

....

....

The participant feels that:

- behaviour is a problem in society
- there is a general lack of respect for authority
- students are disaffected
- changing students' attitudes to school will be hard
- the school hasn't got major behavioural problems
- the school has got disaffected students who have attitude problems and who don't respect the staff
- there should be more discipline in school.

These are our units of meaning. Imagine that the researcher has also interviewed other members of staff and identifies similar units of meaning in their interviews. The researcher can now begin to group the responses together into themes (see Task 11E). This is the second stage of the process.

TASK 11E

What themes might be generated from the units of meaning in Task 11D?

....

....

....

....

TASK 11F

What themes emerge from your research data?

....

....

....

....

You may have identified the following themes:

- the perception of behaviour standards within the school
- the perceived source of behaviour problems
- the attitude of staff towards pupils with behavioural difficulties
- the perceived attitude of staff towards the school's discipline policy.

The third stage of the process requires the researcher to write a narrative that tells the story of each theme and/or tells the story of the participants. The narrative would include quotations from participants to illustrate what the writer is saying. The fourth and final stage is to interpret the data, using your literature review to inform the discussion.

Look at the following example of a research narrative in Figure 11.19. In this narrative the writer has used the interviews, school policy documents and observations. These have then been related to the literature.

Task 11G allows you to try out this approach yourself. In order to work through this process with interview data you will need to transcribe the interview first. You will need to listen to the interview all the way through at least once, to get a sense of what the participant has said. This can also help you to recognise where you have asked leading questions or allowed personal bias to impact upon the interview. At this stage it is a good idea to write a summary of the interview. You will then need to replay the interview several times during transcription. Once you have a transcript it is helpful to read it through to clarify understanding.

Interviews with the pupils revealed that 'time outs', exclusions from the class, were regarded as something worth getting because they allowed the pupils the opportunity to 'opt out' of lessons they didn't like:

> *'Well you can just miss it if you don't like it . . . like when it was the science test and I didn't want to do it I just acted out to Mr B and he, like, said get out and stuff, and I went to student services and looked at the careers stuff which was way better than a test, yeah.'*
>
> *(Jamie, aged 15)*

This contrasted sharply with the view of 'time outs' stated in the policy, which claimed they allowed pupils the opportunity to reflect on their behaviour before returning to the classroom (Somewhere School Behaviour Policy 2004). There was little evidence from the pupils that reflection was a significant part of their 'time out'. Observations within the school confirmed that indeed pupils often wandered the corridors during lesson time, quite legitimately, on the basis of a time out that they had engineered. Some of the teachers who were interviewed expressed doubts about whether a 'time out' worked:

> *'Well it gets them out of your hair, but I don't think they really solve the problems.'*
>
> *(Science teacher, Year 9)*

> *'I try not to use them – it doesn't help really. You don't know where they are . . . you do know they're not in your class learning, which is where they should be.'*
>
> *(Geography teacher, Year 7)*

Friedrickson and Cline (2002) believe that behaviour often results as a result of fight or flight instincts. It could be argued that Jamie's reaction to the science test was a flight which he achieved by securing a time out.

Figure 11.19 Research narrative

TASK 11G

Practice writing a research narrative. Take one theme, identify a quotation from the statistical data you have generated and begin to write your research story.

....

....

....

....

Share your writing with a critical friend and ask them to record what they think. Ask them to consider the following:

• Does the writing make sense to them?
• Have you linked the data to literature?
• Does your quotation/statistical data illustrate the point you want to make?
• Have you referenced correctly?

Interpreting data

You need to be careful of using statistics without giving any thought to what they mean. The interesting issue in relation to the responses to our previous example based on the qualifications held by teaching assistants is, why do so few teaching assistants hold a BA degree? What factors influence a teaching assistant's choice of qualification? It is likely that your analysis of the data will begin to answer some of these questions. Remember that the reason for looking at the data is to find out what it tells us. Statistics can be helpful in allowing us to represent the data we have obtained clearly and simply, but the interpretation of that data goes beyond presentation. It is for you, the researcher, to make sense of the information you have gathered, to link it to your reading and to draw some conclusions. You can see this as a process (Figure 11.20).

Having worked through this guide you should have generated several types of data. These might include observations, interviews

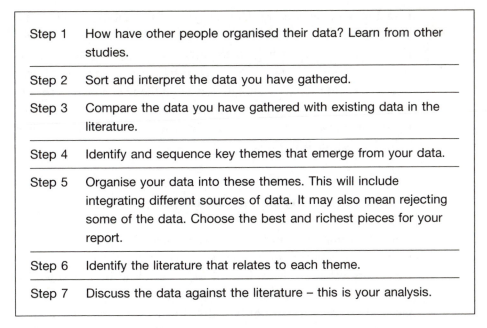

Step 1	How have other people organised their data? Learn from other studies.
Step 2	Sort and interpret the data you have gathered.
Step 3	Compare the data you have gathered with existing data in the literature.
Step 4	Identify and sequence key themes that emerge from your data.
Step 5	Organise your data into these themes. This will include integrating different sources of data. It may also mean rejecting some of the data. Choose the best and richest pieces for your report.
Step 6	Identify the literature that relates to each theme.
Step 7	Discuss the data against the literature – this is your analysis.

Figure 11.20 A seven-step approach to handling research data

or questionnaires. It will include your research diary. It may also include photographic evidence and documentary sources, such as policy documents. You will have conducted thorough background reading into your area, which will help you to see the links between the data you have collected and work already undertaken. Trying to decide which data to use at which point can be a difficult task. There are two key questions:

- What is the data telling me?
- How does this data enhance/prove/justify/reinforce the argument I am making?

You should try to avoid making categorical statements. Don't choose pieces simply because they make a point you believe in. Research is often contradictory. There are arguments and counter arguments. There are often multiple layers of meaning and interpretation. You should endeavour to incorporate a feeling for the complexity of the area in your analysis of the data. By combining quantitative and qualitative data sources into your analysis you will be able to use one to inform the other. This helps in the process of triangulation. In our example on teaching assistants' qualifications we could use the quantitative data on the percentage of people holding different types of qualification and enrich this with qualitative data gained from interviews about why and how people have gained those qualifications.

Validity, reliability and generalisability

Validity is important in research. It enables us to know whether a piece of data accurately describes what it purports to describe. Reliability refers to the ability of the research to be replicated by another researcher. An unreliable item lacks validity but a reliable piece of research might not be valid if it does not measure what it says it is going to measure. There are complex measures of validity, but for a small-scale research project all you need to do is treat your data critically. Ask yourself whether another researcher could replicate your data. You can also ask a friend to critically comment upon the validity of the methods you have chosen to collect your data.

Generalisability refers to the ability of the researcher to make inferences from a small sample to the population as a whole using the research data they have gathered. If your data is representative of the population you are researching you could argue that your findings could be applied to the whole population. In small-scale research it is not possible to gather large amounts of data and true generalisability may not be possible. However, it is possible to relate what you find out from a small sample to the wider population. This is the concept of relatability.

Conclusion

In this chapter we have looked at some simple methods of presenting and interpreting your data. If you are unfamiliar with the mathematical concepts involved in presenting the data you should spend some additional time to familiarise yourself with these basic methods, as they will enrich the quality of your research report. Using such techniques can simplify and clarify key points for your reader. The final stage in carrying out a research project is to write the report. We will look at this in Chapter 12.

Chapter 12
Presenting research findings
Putting it all together

Introduction

You may feel that all of the hard work has been done. You have successfully collected data and analysed it. You know what research story you want to tell. All you have to do now is write the report. In this chapter we will look at how to structure a research report and how to reference correctly, and consider your next steps as a researcher. Bogdan and Biklen (1982: 172) argue that researchers are 'never "ready" to write. Writing is something you must make a conscious decision to do and then discipline yourself to follow through.'

Writing a report

A research report is a form of writing whose purpose is to describe your research story, clearly and accurately. It has a generic text structure that contains:

- a title page
- a contents page
- an introduction
- a literature review
- an outline of your research methods and epistemology
- presentation of your findings
- discussion of your findings
- conclusion
- bibliography
- appendices.

You will be given specific guidance on the structure of your research report. There are generic grammatical features of reports that you should be aware of. These include:

- Research reports tend to focus on generic participants, for example children in general, not Sam the child.

- They use the present tense.

- They use passive constructions. Verbs can be said to have a passive or active construction. The passive construction changes the usual word order to emphasise what happened, rather than who did it. For example:

  - Verb – repair
  - Active construction = I repaired the computer.
  - Passive construction = The computer was repaired.

  We use the passive when we want to create a certain emphasis in our writing. Look at the following example. Here a simple statement is written in two ways. Which is preferable?

  - Active: 'Our pupils followed our advice.' (The emphasis falls on 'our pupils'.)
  - Passive: 'Our advice was followed by our pupils' or 'Our advice was followed.' (The emphasis falls on 'our advice.')

None of these is inherently better than the others: It depends on what you wish to emphasise. You can also use the passive voice when the sentence does not need an 'actor'. For example:

– When the actor is not important – The classroom was heated to 45°.
– When the actor is unknown – The interactive white-board had been stolen.
– When you do not wish to name the actor – One hundred pounds has been donated.

• Research reports tend to use the impersonal voice (third person) – s/he, they, their, his, hers, him, her.
• They use words which generalise – recently, normally, usually, frequently.
• They use technical vocabulary relevant to the subject.
• They use descriptive but factual language.

The writer needs a knowledge of the subject, gained from the literature and from experience and research, in order to write a report that informs the reader. It is important to be clear, so that you do not muddle the reader, and where appropriate to use tables, pictures and diagrams to add more information. After writing you should re-read as if you knew nothing about the subject to check that you have put the information across successfully.

Referencing

When you are writing your report it is essential that you provide detailed and precise information on all the sources you have consulted. You may have used books, journal articles, newspapers, the Internet, government papers, policy documents and statistics. These are the references. Each time you use quotations, or draw upon facts and arguments from one of these sources you need to acknowledge the source. Citing your references also enables the reader to identify the sources you have used. This lets you demon-strate that you are familiar with the relevant material that relates to your research. It also enables someone who is interested in your ideas to find more information. Consistency is essential. There are many styles you can use for citation. One of the most common is the Harvard system, which is outlined in this chapter.

You will use many sources during the course of your research. It is important to maintain a working bibliography that records all of these sources. You need to record the following information.

Books

- name of author or editor (if given in the work) – authors can be persons (e.g. Jerome Bruner), or institutions (e.g. DfES)
- year of publication
- title (in italics)
- edition (if not the first)
- volume number (if a multi-volume work)
- publisher – only given for books, not for journals
- place of publication – only given for books, not for jour-nals.

Journal articles

- name of author of article (if given in the article)
- title of article
- title of journal in full (in italics)
- volume number
- issue number
- year of publication
- the page numbers of the article
- for newspapers, give the date of publication and provide column numbers.

Electronic publications

In addition to the information you gather for a book you must also mention the medium you used to obtain the reference. This is often represented in square brackets, for example [CDROM].

Internet

Where the document is taken from the Internet this statement may be presented as a URL (Uniform Resource Locator). The date on which the information was accessed must be stated. For example:

http://www.standards.dfes.gov.uk/primary/teachingresources/literacy (accessed on 20 June 2001).

Steps to referencing

1   Collect information form the sources you use and compile a working bibliography.
2   Choose a citation system and cite the reference within the text of your work as appropriate.
3   Provide either a reference list or a bibliography at the end of the essay.

Citation in your writing

Any citation within your writing should be linked to the corresponding bibliographic reference at the end of your work. In the text you refer to a particular document by using the author's surname and year of publication. If the author's name occurs naturally in a sentence, the year is given in brackets:

as identified by Bell (2000).

If not, then both name and year are shown in brackets:

> In a recent study (DfES 2002) literacy was described as
> . . .

If the same author has published more than one document in the same year and you have cited both they are identified by lower case letters, e.g. DfES (2001a). If there are two authors both names should be given before the date:

> Cline and Friederickson (2002)

If there are three or more authors only the surname of the first author should be given, followed by *et al.*

> Cohen *et al.* (2000).

Where no author's name is given, use Anon followed by the date.

You may wish to quote a piece of work that has been referred to in something you have read. This generally happens when the original source of the work is not available. You should always reference the source you have read, not the primary source. In the text you should cite the primary source and the source you have read.

> Bee (2000) cites the work of Cline and Friederickson (2002) who
> discuss the impact of fight or flight on behaviour.

Using quotations

A quotation should be accurate to the original. You must include any italics or errors of spelling or punctuation! If the name occurs naturally in your sentence, the year should follow in brackets:

> Bogdan and Biklen (1982: 172) argue that researchers are 'never
> "ready" to write'.

If the name does not occur naturally it and the page number should be shown in brackets.

> It has been suggested that writers are 'never ready to write' (Bogdan and Biklen 1982: 172)

For long quotations (one sentence or more) the quote starts on a new line and is indented, and you don't need to use quotation marks:

> So learners go through:
>
> > definite stages of brain growth, physical growth and development of sensory learning . . . . Piaget's worst legacy is in the education systems using his theories to justify not exposing young children to experiences when their senses are ideally developed to benefit.
> >
> > (Dryden and Vos 1997: 111)

If part of the original text is omitted, indicate this by using full stops in brackets (. . .) in the body of the quotation, or four full stops (. . . .) at the end.

Bibliographies

A bibliography is the list of documents you have read for a specific purpose, in this case your research project. You should prepare a working bibliography for your own use as you conduct your research, even though in the final version you may only cite some of the material. Listing the resources you use as you gather information will save you a lot of time later on.

How to cite in the bibliography

The following sample bibliography shows you how to cite references discussed so far.

DfES (2000) *Curriculum Guidance for the Foundation Stage*. London. DfES.

DfES (2000) *Curriculum Guidance for the Foundation Stage*. London. DfES (online). Available from: http://www.nc. uk.net (Accessed 6 January 2006).

Donaldson, M. (1978) *Children's Minds*. London. Fontana.

UNESCO (1982) *Declaration on Media Education* (online). Available from: http://www.unesco.org/education/pdf/ MEDIA_E.PDF (accessed 6 January 2006).

Remember that if there are two or more authors then all names should be given. If there is a second or later edition, this should be included. If the book has an editor then ed. or eds is added after the name/s and if the publication is part of a series, include that information after the title. Occasionally the person you wish to cite will have made a specific contribution in a book. These should be cited as follows:

Wright, J. A. (1995) 'Provision for children with communication difficulties', in I. Lunt, B. Norwich, J. Wright and M. Kersner *Supporting Children With Communication Problems: sharing the workload*. London. David Fulton Publishers.

If you want to reference a journal article in your bibliography you should cite the version of the article that you have seen. This can be tricky because some journal articles are published in print only, some in print and online (of which some are exact copies and some will appear in a different format), and some online only.

Lozanov, G. (1982) 'Suggestology and suggestopedy', in R. Blair (ed.) *Innovative Approaches to Language Teaching*. Rowley, MA. Newbury House (pp. 14–159).

Glasgow, K.L., Dornbusch, S.M., Troyer, L., Steinberg, L. and Ritter, P.L. (1997) 'Parenting styles, adolescents' attributions, and educational outcomes in nine heterogeneous high schools', *Child Development,* 68 (3), 507–29.

Christenson, P. (2004) 'The health-promoting family: a conceptual framework for future research', *Social Science and Medicine* [online], 59 (2): 223–43. Available from: http://www.sciencedirect.com/science/journal/02779536 (accessed 5 May 2004).

Sandler, M.P. (2003) 'The art of publishing methods', *Journal of Nuclear Medicine* [online], 44: 661–2. Available from: http://jnm.snmjournals.org/content/vol44/issue5/index.shtml (accessed 2 September 2005).

Reference to a news broadcast item:

Eason, G. (2002) BBC News – Teachers reject mum's army, 7 January 2003. Available from: http://news.bbc.co.uk/2/low/uk_news/education/2636565.stm (accessed 14 January 2006).

Reference to a newspaper article:

Fisk, R. (2006) 'Is it him?' *Independent*, 20 January.

If the newspaper appears online then:

Fisk, R. (2006) 'Is it him?' *Independent* (online) 20 January. Available from: http://www.independent.co.uk/ (accessed 21 January 2006).

Reference to a conference paper:

Gunter, H. (2004) *Remodelling the School Workforce*. Paper presented at the School Leadership and Social Justice Seminar Society for Educational Studies. 4 November 2004.

Reference to an Act of Parliament:

Great Britain. Parliament (2002) Care Standards Act 2002. London. The Stationery Office.

Reference to a website:

In the text:

> Staffordshire University has a helpful guide to referencing.
> Further information can be obtained from its website
> (Staffordshire University 2006a)

In the reference list:

> Staffordshire University (2006a) Staffordshire University (online).
> Available from: http://www.staffs.ac.uk (accessed 20
> January 2006).

Reference to a CD-ROM:

> Department for Education and Skills (2000) 'A breath of fresh air:
> an interactive guide to managing breathlessness in patients
> with lung cancer' [CD Rom]. Sutton: Institute of Cancer
> Research.

Where next?

When you have completed your research you will probably be very self-critical. There will have been aspects of the research that you will feel you could have done better. It is quite natural to feel like this and you should reflect upon the experience of doing research in your written report. You may also feel that your research is incomplete. Much research generates new questions or areas for further investigation. Indeed your research may not fully answer the question you originally posed. It is important to share your research with other people. Many foundation degrees include the opportunity to present your research at a seminar or mini-conference. It is important that you engage in this process. What you have discovered from your research will help others answer questions about the context. You should also make sure that you provide access to your research to all those who are entitled to see it. This could include your colleagues, managers and your participants, if this was agreed as part of the research process.

Conclusion

In this chapter we have looked at how to structure a research report and how to reference correctly. We have discussed the importance of sharing your research. What is clear is that as a result of having done research you will have developed some important skills that will help you in your professional and personal development. Congratulations on successfully completing your first research project!

References

Bales, R.F. (1950) *Interaction Process Analysis: A Method for the Study of Small Group.* Cambridge, MA. Addison-Wesley.

Bell, J. (1999) *Doing your Research Project.* Maidenhead. Open University Press.

Blatchford, I. (ed.) *Doing Early Childhood Research: International Perspectives on Theory and Practice.* Buckingham. Open University Press.

Bogdan, R.C. and Biklen, S.K. (1982) *Qualitative Research for Education: An Introduction to Theory and Methods.* Boston, MA. Allyn & Bacon.

Booth, T. and Ainscow, M. (2004) *Index for Inclusion: Developing Learning, Participation and Play in Early Years and Childcare.* Bristol. Centre for Studies in Inclusive Education.

Borg, W.R. (1981) *Applying Educational Research: A Practical Guide for Teachers.* New York. Longman.

Boud, D., Keough, R. and Walker, D. (1985) *Reflection: Turning Experience into Learning.* London. Kogan Page.

Brooker, L. (2001) 'Interviewing Children'. In MacNaughton, G., Rolfe, S. and Siraj-Blatchford, I. (eds) *Doing Early Childhood Research: International Perspectives on Theory and Practice.* Crows Nest, NSW. Allen and Unwin.

Campbell, A., McNamara, O. and Gilroy, P. (2004) *Practitioner and Professional Development in Education.* London. Paul Chapman Publishing.

Carr, W. and Kemmis, S. (1986) *Becoming Critical: Education, Knowledge and Action Research*. Lewes. Falmer.

Cicourel, A.V. (1964) *Method and Measurement in Sociology*. New York. The Free Press.

Clough, P. and Nutbrown, C. (2002) *A Student's Guide to Methodology*. London. Sage Publications.

Cohen, L., Manion, L. and Morrison, K. (2000) *Research Methods in Education*. London. Routledge Falmer.

Connolly, P. (1998) *Racism, Gender Identities and Young Children: Social Relations in a Multi-Ethnic, Inner-City Primary School*. London. Routledge.

Denscombe, M. (2003) *The Good Research Guide*. Maidenhead. Open University Press.

Department for Education and Skills (DfES) (2004) The Children Bill. London. HMSO.

Department for Education and Skills (DfES) Children's and Young People's Unit (CYPU) (2001) *Core Principles for the Involvement of Children and Young People*. Nottingham. DfES Publications.

Dewey, J. (1933) *How We Think*. Chicago. Henrey Regney.

Drew, C.J. (1980) *Introduction to Designing and Conducting Research,* 2nd edition. Missouri, MO. C.B. Mosby Company.

Drummond, M.J. (2002) 'Listening to Children Talking'. Online. Available HTTP: <http://66.249.93.104/search?q=cache:rybo6XmtNhwJ:www.ncb. org.uk/resources/Nottingham_Early_Years_Conference_2002_Report.pdf +Drummond,+M.J.+(2002)+%E2%80%98Listening+to+Children+Talking %E2%80%99+&hl=en&ct=clnk&cd=2> (accessed 2 May 2006).

Elliot, J. (1991) *Action Research for Educational Change*. Buckingham. Open University Press.

Eraut, M. (1994) *Developing Professional Knowledge and Competence*. London. Falmer Press.

Field, P.A. and Morse, J.M. (1989) *Nursing Research: The Application of Qualitative Methods*. London. Chapman and Hall.

Flanders, N.A. (1970) *Analysing Teacher Behaviour*. Cambridge, MA. Addison-Wesley.

Friedrickson, N. and Cline, T. (2002). *Special Educational Needs: Inclusion and Diversity*. London. OUP.

Great Britain. Parliament (1989) The Children Act 1989. London. The Stationery Office.

Great Britain. Parliament (1995a) The Children (Northern Ireland) Order 1995. London. The Stationery Office.

Great Britain. Parliament (1995b) The Children (Scotland) Act 1995. London: The Stationery Office.

Great Britain. Parliament (1999) Child Protection Act 1999. London. The Stationery Office.

Grebenik, E. and Moser, C.A. (1962) 'Society: problems and methods of study'. In Welford, A.T., Argyle, M., Glass, O. and Morris, J.N. (eds) *Statistical Surveys.* London. Routledge & Kegan Paul.

Howard, K. and Sharp, J.A. (1983) *The Management of a Student Research Project.* Aldershot. Gower.

Kemmis, S. (1997) 'Action research'. In Keeves, J.P. (ed.) *Educational Research, Methodology, and Measurement: An International Handbook,* 2nd edition. Oxford. Elsevier Science Ltd.

Kemmis, S. (1985). 'Action research and the politics of reflection'. In Boud, D., Keogh, R. and Walker, D. (eds.) *Reflection: Turning Experience into Learning.* London. Kogan Page.

Kemmis, S. and McTaggart, R. (eds) (1990). *The Action Research Reader.* Victoria. Deakin University Press.

Kemmis, S. and McTaggart, R. (eds) (1992) *The Action Research Planner,* 3rd edition. Victoria. Deakin University Press.

Kerlinger, F.N. (1970) *Foundations of Behavioural Research.* New York. Holt, Rinehart and Winston.

Kirby, P., Lanyon, C., Cronin, K. and Sinclair, R. (2003) *Building a Culture of Participation. Involving Children and Young People in Policy, Service Planning, Development and Evaluation: A Research Report.* London. DES.

Kitwood, T.M. (1977) 'Values in adolescent life: towards a critical description'. Unpublished Ph.D. dissertation. School of Education, University of Bradford.

Kolb, D.A. (1984) *Experiential Learning.* Englewood Cliffs, NJ. Prentice Hall.

Kvale, S. (1996) *Interviews.* London. Sage.

Lancaster, Y. and Broadbent, V. (2003) *Listening to Young Children.* Maidenhead. Open University Press/McGraw Hill Publishing Company.

Langeveld, M.J. (1965) 'In search of research'. In *Paedagogica Europoea: The European Year Book of Educational Research,* Vol. 1. Amsterdam. Elsevier.

Lather, P. (1991) *Getting Smart: Feminist Research and Pedagogy with/in the Postmodern.* London. Sage Publications.

Lewin, K. (1946) 'Action research and minority problems'. *Journal of Social Issues* 2: 34–46.

Lewin, K. (1948) *Resolving Social Conflicts*. New York. Harper.

Lewin, K. and Grabbe, P. (1945) 'Conduct, knowledge and acceptance of new values'. *Journal of Social Issues* 2: 53–63.

Lewis, A. (1992) 'Group child interviews as a research tool'. *British Educational Research Journal* 18 (4): 413–21.

Macintyre, C. (2002) *The Art of the Action Research in the Classroom.* London. David Fulton.

MacNaughton, G., Rolfe, S. and Siraj-Blatchford, I. (eds) (2001) *Doing Early Childhood Research: International Perspectives on Theory and Practice.* Buckingham. Open University Press.

McTaggart, R. (1996) 'Issues for participatory action researchers'. In Zuber-Skerrit, O. (ed.) *New Directions in Action Research*. London. Falmer.

Mezirow, J. (1981) 'A critical theory of adult learning and education'. *Adult Education* 32 (1): 3–24.

Miller, C. 1995) 'In depth interviewing by telephone: some practical considerations'. *Evaluation and Research in Education* 9 (1): 29–38.

Morgan, N. and Saxton, J. (1991). *Teaching, Questioning and Learning.* London. Routledge.

Morrow, V. and Richards, M. (1996) 'The ethics of social research with children: an overview'. *Children and Society* 10: 90–105.

Moser, C.A. and Kalton, G. (1971) *Survey Methods in Social Investigation*, 2nd edition. London. Heinemann.

National Children's Bureau (2002) 'Including children in social research'. *Highlight* No: 193.

Nisbet, J.D. (1977) 'Small-scale research: guidelines and suggestions for development'. *Scottish Educational Studies* 9, May: 13–17.

Nixon, J. (1981) *A Teacher's Guide to Action Research*. London. Grant McIntyre.

Oppenheim, A.N. (1992) *Questionnaire Design and Attitude Measurement.* London. Heinemann.

Reid, B. (1993) '"But we're doing it already": Exploring a response to the concept of reflective practice in order to improve its facilitation', *Nurse Education Today* 13: 305-9.

Roberts-Holmes, G. (2005) *Doing Your Early Years Research Project: a Step by Step Guide*. London. Paul Chapman Publishing.

Schön, D.A. (1983). *The Reflective Practitioner: How Professionals Think in Action.* New York. Basic Books.

Simons, H. (1982) 'Conversation piece: the practice of interviewing in case study research'. In McCormick, R. (ed.) *Calling Education to Account.* London. Heinemann.

SPSS (1990a) *SPSS Categories*. Chicago, IL. SPSS Inc.

SPSS (1990b) *SPSS User's Guide*. Chicago, IL. SPSS Inc.

Stringer, E.T. (1999) *Action Research: A Handbook for Practitioners*, 2nd edition. Newbury Park, CA. Sage.

Stringer, E.T. (2003) *Action Research in Education*. Newbury Park, CA. Prentice Hall.

Sudman, S. and Bradburn, N.M. (1982) *Asking Questions: A Practical Guide to Questionnaire Design*. San Francisco, CA. Jossey-Bass Inc.

Trist, E. (1979) *Referent Organizations and the Development of Inter-Organizational Domains*. 39th Annual Convention of the Academy of Management (Atlanta, 09.08.79), 23–4.

Trist, E.L. and Sofer, C. (1959) *Exploration in Group Relations*. Conference held 1957 by University of Leicester and the Tavistock Institute of Human Relations. Leicester University.

United Nations (1989) *Convention on the Rights of the Child*. General Assembly Resolution A/RES/44/25 (Passed 12 December). Online. Available HTTP: <http://www.hri.org/docs/CRC89.html> (accessed 2 May 2006).

Usher, R., Bryant, I. and Johnston, R. (1997) *Adult Education and the Postmodern Challenge: Learning Beyond the Limits*. London. Routledge.

Watts, M. and Ebbutt, D. (1987) 'More than the sum of the parts: research methods in group interviewing'. *British Educational Research Journal* 13 (1): 25–34.

Webb, G. (1996) 'Becoming critical of action research'. In Zuber-Skerrit, O. (ed.) *New Directions in Action Research*. London. Falmer.

Weedon, C. (1987) *Feminist Practice and Poststructuralist Theory*. Oxford. Blackwell.

Whyte, W.F. (1982) 'Interviewing in field research'. In Burgess, R. (ed.) *Field Research: A Sourcebook and Field Manual*. London. George Allen & Unwin.

Wilson, N. and MacLean, S. (1994) *Questionnaire Design: A Practical Introduction*. Newtown Abbey, Co. Antrim. University of Ulster Press.

Winter, R. (1987) *Action Research and the Nature of Social Inquiry: Professional Innovation and Educational Work*. Aldershot. Gower.

Winter, R. (1989) *Learning From Experience. Principles and Practice in Action Research*. Lewes. Falmer Press.

Winter, R (1996) 'Some principles and procedures for the conduct of action research', in Zuber-Skerritt, O. (ed.) *New Directions in Action Research*. London. Falmer Press.

Wiseman, J.P. and Aron, M.S. (1972) *Field Reports in Sociology.* London. Transworld Publishers.

Woods, P. (1986) *Inside Schools: Ethnography in Educational Research.* London. Routledge & Kegan Paul.

Zuber-Skerritt, O. (1982) *Action Research in Higher Education.* London. Kogan Page.

Zuber-Skerritt, O. (ed.) (1996) *New Directions in Action Research.* London. Falmer Press.

Index

Please note that any page references to non-textual material such as Figures are in *italic* print